CO-AAM-130

1000 PATHS TO PERFECT GOLF

1000 PATHS TO PERFECT GOLF

STEPHEN WILKINSON

My gratitude to all those great players whom I quote—and especially to my dear life partner, Claudia, for encouraging me to make her a golfing widow and thereby turning me into the happiest middle-aged kid in the world.

About the Author

Born in Nottinghamshire, England in 1956, Stephen Wilkinson is an author, journalist, translator, and academic with a PhD in Cuban Literature.

CONTENTS

INTRODUCTION

In the summer of 2000 at the age of 43, and acting entirely on a whim, I went to a nearby golf driving range and began to hit golf balls. I was a sorry sight; as anyone who has ever tried golf for the first time knows, you miss far more often than you hit. But when you do manage to send that little white ball soaring, the elation is astonishing—addiction is only another firm blow away.

The next week, I bought a set of clubs at a yard sale and on the first free afternoon I had, I went to a local pay-and-play course. I returned home frustrated but determined to get better. Although I was truly awful, I had become hooked and I was resolved to learn how to play this wonderful, exasperating, and ultimately unfathomable game.

I had lessons, practiced on the range, and played whenever I could. I read avidly, watched golf on TV, and tried everything and anything that offered me the hope of improvement. The results speak for themselves. For here I am, three years on from picking up a club, playing off an official handicap of five.

And so we come to this book. Let me say straight off that this is not a book of instruction, for there are those with far better credentials than I have to teach you how to play. Nor is it a book that professes to have the secret that will turn you into Tiger Woods overnight. No, if anything, as you will find within these pages, the hardest lesson of all to learn is that there are no secrets to good golf.

This book is a collection of wisdom: 1000 good ideas, pieces of advice, tips on technique, and pearls of knowledge that I have found helpful along the way. It assumes that you play right-handed, as I do, so please accept my apologies if you are left-handed—no doubt you can swap the references to right and left when you come upon them. However, whichever way you play the game, I hope that this book will help you to improve your scores and put you on the path to enjoying a perfect round of golf.

OPENING SHOTS

1 As to the question of "Why play golf?" I would suggest a similar answer "Why not play golf?" Anyone can do it.

[GARY PLAYER]

2 On the golf course, a man may be the dogged victim of inexorable fate, be struck down by an appalling stroke of tragedy, become the hero of unbelievable melodrama, or the clown in a sidesplitting comedy.

[BOBBY JONES]

3 Golf presents demands unlike those of any other sport.

4 To reach your potential you must refine your talent.

5 **Look for a teacher who communicates well, is on your wavelength, and with whom you can be friends—then stick with them.**

6 Even though golf is now flooded by gadgets, gimmicks, products, and myriad philosophies, it is basically the same game it was in days of old.

7 Exercise is a proven and fun way to reduce stress and improve your overall conditioning, and golf is an increasingly popular way to exercise.

8 The challenge is to untangle all the available information and find a path that suits you.

9 There is no shape nor size of body, no awkwardness nor ungainliness, which puts good golf beyond reach. There are good golfers with spectacles, with one eye, with one leg, even with one arm. In golf, while there is life, there is hope.

[SIR WALTER SIMPSON]

10 **To succeed, combine your talent with discipline, hard work, and diligence.**

11 Play on a variety of courses—this will ensure you have a bank of shots.

12 **Golf shots are like pebbles on the beach, they all have the same basic characteristic but each one is unique.**

13 Confidence, of course, is an admirable asset to a golfer, but it should be an unspoken confidence. It is perilous to put into speech. The gods of golf lie in wait to chasten the presumptuous.

[P. G. WOODHOUSE]

14 **Play in all conditions—the fair weather golfer is not a real golfer.**

15 Give it a rest from time to time.

16 Commit yourself to all your shot decisions.

17 Golf is a solitary pursuit and requires introspection.

18 Learning the correct movements is 10 times easier than you think; doing things the right way takes a lot less effort than the wrong way.

[BEN HOGAN]

19 Focused concentration is essential in golf.

20 Anyone can hit a great shot on the range, but doing it in competition is what counts.

21 You must exercise to improve your golf and prevent injury.

22 To improve your golf you must train, prepare, and practice as the winners do.

23 Devise a golf training plan.

24 Those who believe that talent is enough to guarantee their best performance are destined to fail.

[GARY PLAYER]

25 Set yourself a few realistic goals along the path to your ultimate target.

26 **The journey is the process by which you arrive at your end result.**

27 "One lesson £1,000. Five lessons £150. If you want a miracle you will have to pay for it."
—Sign in a pro shop window.

28 **No matter how badly you are playing you could always play worse.**

29 No matter how well you are playing you can always do better.

30 You only need a five on every hole to score 90.

31 Once upon a time a bogey was considered a good score.

32 The stories about bad scores rarely start with "I hit one down the middle."

[COLIN MONTGOMERIE]

33 Par is the professional's scale of performance—shooting par for the weekend golfer is like running the 100 meters in 10 seconds.

34 What is a good score for you? That is your target for average performance.

35 If you hit the ball 150 yards off the tee, play the 300-yard holes as par fives.

36 Don't let one shot cost you two.

37 Never hit a shot you haven't practiced.

38 The spirit of golf is to dare a hazard, and in negotiating it, reap a reward.

[GEORGE C. THOMAS]

39 **Keep your ego in check.**

40 The driver used to be called "the play club"—it was a club you used to put the ball in play.

41 **Seek the level ground.**

42 You only need two good shots a hole to make a par.

43 It sometimes makes sense to play aggressively, but it always makes sense to play smart.

[JIM FLICK]

44 Golfers should not live by results alone.

45 In the fairway of life, take time to smell the roses; you only get to play one round.

[BEN HOGAN]

46 **Find out what you need to learn, how to learn it, and then develop methods that will help you achieve your goals.**

[DAVE PELZ]

47 Golf is a number of different games in one: You have to putt, you have to play delicate chips, and you have to hit powerful drives. But then you have to learn how to play the course and, hardest of all, master your own emotions.

48 What others may find in poetry or an art museum, I find in the flight of a good drive.

[ARNOLD PALMER]

49 **Read books, watch videos, study the game—it is not only learned on the battlefield.**

50 Golf is a long-term relationship, but the game is a lover as fickle as she is enchanting.

[BEN HOGAN]

51 **In golf, a little knowledge is a dangerous thing and complete ignorance leads to bewilderment.**

52 Take lessons, practice, and learn.

53 Golf is a way of testing ourselves while enjoying ourselves.

[ARNOLD PALMER]

54 Undulation is the soul of golf.

[H. M. WETHERED]

55 It is almost impossible to hit a pure golf shot.

56 Build your game from green to tee—not the other way around.

57 **If all your shots were perfect you wouldn't know the meaning of perfect.**

58 The hole-in-one is proof that good things happen for reasons we don't know.

59 Golf is game where invariably things cannot be addressed directly, but by directing attention to something else.

[BOBBY JONES]

60 A fine golf shot is succinct, simple, unambiguous, and indisputable and creates such sheer joy that once you've hit one, you can't wait to hit another.

61 **Golf should be learned starting from the cup and progressing back to the tee.**

[HARVEY PENICK]

62 If you play golf just for the exercise—there are better ways to exercise.

63 **If you play golf just for the fun of it—there are better ways to have fun.**

64 **If you play golf just for the challenge to master it—give up now because you never will.**

65 Remember: The rough is only a less desirable lie.

66 To get the most out of golf learn to appreciate its elusive nature.

67 **The natural, logical way to learn golf is to start with the shortest swing and increase to the full swing.**

[TOM WATSON]

68 Choose your home golf course wisely. Does it have a practice ground? Is it close to home? Is it very busy? All these factors will affect your capacity to improve and enjoy the game.

69 **The essential traits of a good golfer are: patience, resilience, clarity, curiosity, and talent.**

[GARY PLAYER]

70 You will hardly ever lose a ball through no fault of your own.

71 **The first thing you should do when you see your ball in a divot is accept it happens to everyone, but you might resolve never to leave a divot unrepaired yourself.**

[KEN VENTURI]

72 You will learn to love your golf course, and there will always be one you call home.

73 **There are always friends waiting on the first tee.**

74 Every round of golf is the opportunity to start again.

75 **The score is important, of course. And the discovery that you are superior to another golfer is satisfying. But when your score is bad and the other fellow beats you, golf still has been a blessing to you. The score isn't the be-all and end-all.**

[TOMMY ARMOUR]

76 Take what the game deals you and keep on moving forward.

77 **Learn from a qualified coach.**

78 Though it sounds paradoxical, good golf is much easier to play than poor golf. Certainly it is more pleasant.

[PATTY BERG]

79 **Double check your card at the end of the round.**

80 Use the best equipment for you.

81 Shape up your mind and body for good golf.

82 It is utterly impossible for any golfer to play good golf without a swing that will repeat.

[BEN HOGAN]

83 **Believe your body knows how to hit the right shot.**

84 This is my attitude to my favorite game. I have its honor to support. So has each one who enters its fold. An error in count, an error that moves the ball, an error that in any way makes you take improper advantage over your opponent, seen or unseen, is the worst error in the whole game. We begin each hole with the question, "Who has the honor?"

[GLENNA COLLETT VARE]

85 The next shot will be better.

86 There is no miracle that cannot happen at least once in golf.

[GRANTLAND RICE]

87 There is no trouble that you can't get out of in one shot—even if it's a penalty.

88 Everyone hits a bad shot sometimes. You will hit your share of great ones to make up for them.

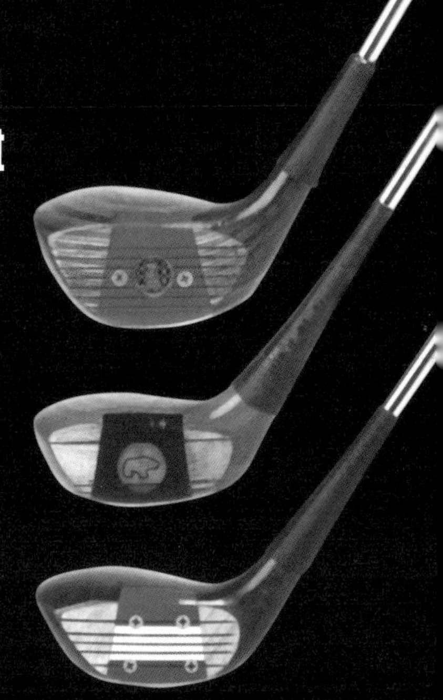

89 Golf is a game of a lifetime. Not because you can play for your lifetime, but because it takes a lifetime to master.

[BILL STRAUSBAUGH]

90 **A bunker is a place for atonement.**

[HARRY VARDON]

91 **Water is the least desirable lie.**

92 The greatest pleasure is obtained by improving.

[BEN HOGAN]

93 **Trust your subconscious to know what to do.**

94 You can always make up one shot.

95 Always have a goal in golf and always expect to achieve it.

96 There's nothing difficult about golf, the average golfer, if he goes about it intelligently, should play in the 70s.

[BEN HOGAN]

97 Golf is a game that needlessly prolongs the life of some of our most useless citizens.

[BOB HOPE]

98 **There is no doubt that doubt is your worst enemy.**

99 Make a point of remembering the great putts you have holed.

100 If you cannot see the shot in your mind's eye, you will rarely see it for real.

101 Believe you can do it and you will.

102 No matter how good we may be, if we should fancy that we have mastered the game to the extent that we can go out day after day and play as we please, then we are greater fools than ought to be left at large.

[BOBBY JONES]

103 **Never play your shot out of turn. The person farthest from the pin plays first.**

104 Don't know whose honor it is on the tee? At the start the lowest handicapper has the honor, after that the person who had the lowest gross score on the last hole goes first.

105 Always mark your ball on the green if it obstructs your opponent's putt.

106 Shake hands when the game is over.

107 Watch where your opponent's ball lands.

108 Let a group through if you are holding them up.

109 Golf shoes must be worn at all times. Never wear trainers.

110 Stay for the awards even if you haven't won.

111 Dress smart to play smart.

112 In match play, give your opposition putts that are under a foot long unless a putt will win the hole or match.

113 Offer to attend the flag for your opponent on the green.

114 Announce the score after each hole to prevent mistakes.

115 When marking a card, write down both your score and your opponent's score after each hole to ensure accuracy.

116 Remember to sign both your card and your opponent's card.

117 Tip your caddy something extra if you have paid for his service at the clubhouse.

118 Turn off your mobile phone when on the course.

119 You must buy the drinks if you get a hole-in-one.

120 Keep up with the speed of the course—a round of golf shouldn't take all day.

121 Help your opponent look for a lost ball.

122 Never stand behind your opponent in the line with their shot.

123 **Don't talk loudly or shout because you can be heard on other holes.**

124 Replace your divots and repair pitch marks on the greens.

125 Offer to attend the flagstick for your partner when putting.

126 **When attending the stick, avoid letting your shadow fall across your partner's line.**

127 Don't let the end of the flagstick damage the green.

128 Carry a book of rules in your bag.

129 Rake bunkers after use—including areas that others have left unraked.

130 Never take your cart onto the tee or putting green.

131 Be ready to play your shot.

132 Why not insure yourself against getting a hole-in-one?

133 Like pool, golf is primarily a game of position.

[ROBERT TRENT JONES, JR.]

134 Many courses don't allow metal spiked golf shoes.

135 If wearing shorts, men often need to wear long socks and they usually have to be white.

136 Avoid taking too much time at address—it irritates your partners.

137 Jacket and tie for men is usually required in the clubhouse.

138 Collared shirts are essential at most courses.

139 **Try to keep up with the game in front, not stay ahead of the game behind.**

GRIPPING IT AND RIPPING IT

140 **Good golf begins with a good grip.**

[BEN HOGAN]

141 Some good players have poor grips but no poor player has a good grip.

142 The last three fingers of the left hand hold the club firmly like a good handshake, while the index, thumb, and right hand are applied lightly as if holding a child's hand.

143 Rate your grip pressure on a scale of one to 10, with one being super-light and 10 being super-tight. Hit shots using each pressure in turn. You will soon discover the number that produces your best swing. It will probably be in the four to five range.

144 Quiet hands respond on their own to the weight of the clubhead. Tight hands have to be told what to do.

[JIM FLICK]

145 Make sure your hands are in a neutral position—the palms must face each other.

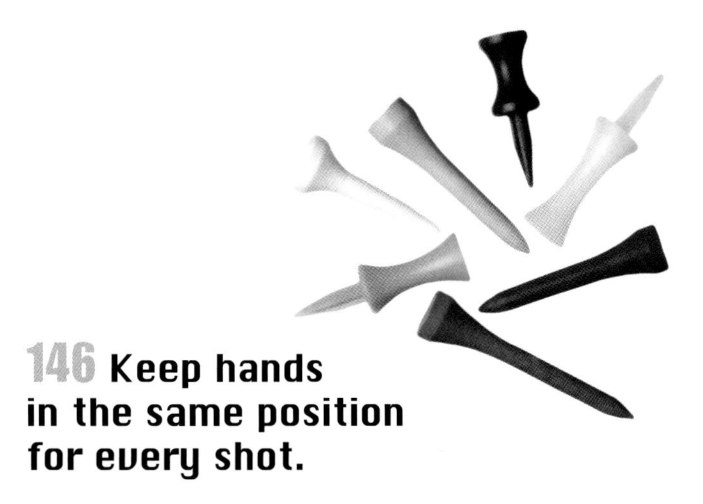

146 Keep hands in the same position for every shot.

147 Keep consistent pressure on your grip.

148 The correct grip should be the first thing learned. But once learned it should not be changed.

[BOBBY JONES]

149 If you have a strong grip (more than two knuckles showing of the left hand when you look down at your hands on address) that feels too uncomfortable when you try to neutralize it, you may be gripping too much with your fingers. Try laying the club across the palm where the fingers meet the hands and grip the club.

150 Always align yourself correctly.

151 **Ball position on long shots is crucial.**

152 If you discover a feeling at address that produces a correct result, memorize it and aim to reproduce it every time.

153 Contrary to the commonly held wisdom, it is not always a good idea to move the ball forward in your stance to hit it higher.

154 To get the ball in the center of your stance, address it with your feet together and then part them equally on either side of the ball.

155 **Before you swing, you should be relaxed but ready.**

156 As you start the backswing, be aware of feeling passive and relaxed in your arms and upper body but springy on your legs.

157 Feel your body coiling like a spring on the backswing.

158 When addressing the ball, think 50-50 while balancing your weight evenly on both feet.

159 A good golf swing requires an element of faith in the self that will allow you to release the body into the hitting area with a movement beyond that which your fears would prefer you to stop.

[TIMOTHY O'GRADY]

160 Square your stance by laying a club on the ground pointing at the target, then butt your toes against it. Practice like this.

161 Try to keep your shoulders parallel with your feet.

162 **To get into the correct posture: Hold your club straight out in front of you, horizontal to the ground. Keep your knees flexed, and tilt your spine forward from the hips until the club touches the ground.**

163 Don't be stiff legged—keep knees soft.

164 At address you should feel as though you are sitting on a shooting stick.

165 To get the correct feeling of weight distribution, stand tall as you normally would and feel where the weight is—it should be evenly spread between the ball and heel. This is exactly how it should be when you address the ball.

166 A golfer who learns to swing hard initially can usually acquire accuracy later, whereas a golfer who gets too accuracy-conscious at the outset will rarely be able to make himself hit the ball hard later on.

[JACK NICKLAUS]

167 **To check the correct weight distribution, you should be able to curl your toes up in your shoes without losing balance.**

168 To be sure you are aiming correctly, picture a set of railroad tracks leading to the target. The track furthest from you should be where the golf ball lies, while the track closest should be where you butt up your feet.

169 To help weight transfer during the shot, slant your lead foot a little toward the target.

170 To help focus your mind, develop a pre-shot routine and stick to it: Stand behind the ball, choose your target, and take a practice swing while visualizing the ball's flight to the target. Now, address the ball lining up the clubface, look at the target once again, and swing through the ball with the same tempo as on your practice swing.

171 The width of your stance should be about the same width as your shoulders.

172 **The common denominator for all golfers is tempo, so I advise every golfer, no matter their skill level, to think tempo—the smooth transition from backswing to downswing—as the primary swing thought.**

[HALE IRWIN]

173 Irons are better played with the ball at the center and rear of center of your stance to allow a hit in the downward part of the swing arc.

174 **Woods are better played with the ball left of center of your stance to give the feel of sweeping at the ball.**

175 **Good balance is essential in developing a good swing.**

176 There is no one perfect ball position because everyone has a different height, weight, and flexibility.

177 With your four to eight irons, play the ball halfway between your inside left heel and the center of your stance.

178 If the ball is positioned too far back in the stance you could pull it.

179 **With your nine iron and wedges play the ball in the middle of your stance.**

180 Good posture enables you to stay balanced throughout the swing.

181 **A wide stance can restrict movement.**

182 **Bend your knees to create greater flexibility of movement.**

183 A narrow stance can affect balance.

184 At address you should have a feeling that your tailbone is being lifted up. There should be slight tension in the small of the back as you raise your bottom.

185 **Try to keep a "tail up" feeling throughout the swing.**

186 The spine angle will be marginally different from club to club due to the difference in shaft length.

187 Aim the clubface first, then position your feet.

188 Raise your head slightly so your chin is off your chest.

189 Good grip and stance are so vital that if either is incorrect, pros can foresee what will go wrong before you make the swing.

190

Try to waggle before the back swing, forming the habit of blending it into the start of the swing—this helps you to relax and get into position.

191

The waggle gives the golfer a running start. It blends right into the swing. For all general points and purposes, the backswing is simply an extension of the way the golfer takes the club back on the waggle.

[BEN HOGAN]

192 Practice swinging within yourself—trying too hard can destroy balance and rhythm.

193 With your driver, woods, two, and three irons, play the ball just inside of your left heel.

194 **Don't pick up the club—swing it.**

195 Don't drop the right shoulder during the downswing.

196 Think of the right shoulder passing under the left as you strike through the ball.

197 Try to develop a feeling that the left hand is pulling the clubhead down.

198 Swing—don't hit.

199 A hit must be perfectly timed, but a swing will time itself.

[GRANTLAND RICE]

200 It is very rare that tension is observed in a practice swing and this is so because the player, not feeling the necessity of being entirely correct, comes closer to assuming a natural posture. Let him take this naturalness into the actual shot; let him simplify his preliminary motions as much as possible; and let him start the ball on its way without hurry.

[BOBBY JONES]

201 Think 'low and slow' as you take the club away.

202 On your followthrough, think "waist to face the target."

203 **Think "weight on the right side" as you start to make the downswing.**

204 Imagine you are standing on a clockface with your feet aligned towards 12 o'clock as you address the ball. Think of swinging through in the direction of two o'clock as you hit it.

205 Lifting your head during the shot is usually the result of another fault and not the actual cause of a poor shot.

206 **Resist the tendency for your eye to follow the clubhead as it goes back away from the ball.**

207 Too short a backswing leads to short shots.

208 **Learn to swing the club without using the wrists.**

209 Swing thoughts do work, but no one swing thought will work for long—change them frequently.

210 When you are struggling during a round, take several practice swings until you get it to look, sound, and feel correct again.

211 **Let your body, not your hands and arms, control the pace of your downswing and followthrough.**

212 **Your belly button should be facing the target when you finish.**

213 Turn your shoulders back and through the ball.

214 For a completed backswing, your lead shoulder should be under your chin at the top.

215 **A common flaw is to swing at the ball when you really want to swing along a plane where the ball just happens to be.**

216 Having timing problems? Try swinging a heavy broom. The heaviness will teach your body to make the most efficient weight transfer and keep weight balanced.

217 Develop a powerful pivot: Take your normal stance and then pull your front foot back away from the target line and lift your heel off the ground. Keep the heel off the ground as you make your backswing. You will end up with most of your weight over the back leg, which is the perfect position from which to unwind powerfully through impact.

218 Swing 'oily'.

[RAYMOND FLOYD]

219 Get the feeling of shifting your weight to the back foot during your backswing.

220 On the downswing, start to transfer your weight just ahead of the club.

221 When you stroke with timing and rhythm, the ball sails straight down the fairway and for a distance. It is effortless power, not powerful effort.

[ERNEST JONES]

222 Always pick a target before adopting your stance. Choose a spot a few feet in front of you on the ground along the target line and set up square to that.

223 Check if your head bobs up and down during your swing. Have a friend place a club lightly on your head during a practice swing. You will soon feel the movement.

224 Ben Hogan insisted on angling the left foot out slightly and keeping the back foot square to the target line.

225 Tiger Woods flares his right foot out because the turn he makes puts so much strain on his right knee.

226 Letting the left heel rise is not a bad thing.

227 Work on getting your wrists set early. Try to get your wrists fully hinged by the time the club is at waist height. From here, all you have to do is complete the shoulder turn to get the clubhead into the perfect position at the top.

228 **Tilt your head slightly to the right at address, to help you remain back behind the ball.**

229 Concentrate on looking at the ball with your left eye throughout the entire backswing and downswing.

230 Resist the natural tendency to swing the arms independently of the body.

231 Nobody ever swung a club too slowly.

[BOBBY JONES]

232 Synchronize your body and arms by practicing only half swings, concentrating on keeping the arms in unison with the body. On the backswing, turn your belly button away from the ball and do not break the wrists. On the followthrough ensure your hands finish shoulder height and the waist turns toward the target.

233 Keep your chin away from your chest throughout the swing.

234 Hover the clubhead above the ground at address to prevent the club's snagging on the ground or in the grass on the takeaway.

235 **Commit yourself to a full shoulder turn.**

236 Visualize the spine as a fixed axle around which your body, shoulders, and arms must rotate.

237 Great players work hard to find a tempo that suits them and then try to maintain that throughout the range of their shots.

238 The hands are the key to transmitting power from the body to the club. The club shaft is held more in the fingers than the palms of your hands. In the palm, it is impossible to get any zip into the shot.

[SAM SNEAD]

239 Try hitting practice shots with your feet together. Make as full a swing as you can without losing balance. This teaches the relative importance of your upper to lower body.

240 You can't define rhythm, you have to feel it.

241 **When you are swinging with rhythm you know it.**

242 Harvey Penick believed the best swing thought was to think of allowing your weight to shift onto your front foot just as the right elbow returns to the side of the body on the downswing.

243 At the start of the backswing, Tiger Woods says he thinks of extending the butt end of the club away from the right hip as far as possible in order to create a good wide turn.

244 To get the right extension through impact, imagine there is a second ball six inches ahead of your ball along the target line. Try to "hit" this second ball as well as the real one.

245 **Try to get the left shoulder to turn behind the ball at the top of the backswing.**

246 **If you have trouble activating your legs on the downswing, try consciously "kicking" the left knee toward the target on the downswing.**

247 You have a natural beat—time yourself walking and see what cadence you have. If you walk briskly, your natural golf rhythm will be brisk too. If you are a stroller, you will be a slower swinger.

248 To improve your swing tempo, practice hitting balls with a backswing length and wrist break that are governed by stopping the backswing at the point at which the end of the club grip points downward directly at the ball. This should be just short of horizontal.

249 **All the great players from Bobby Jones on were convinced that the first movement of the downswing should be the hips sliding slightly toward the left.**

250 It was said that Bobby Jones could hit balls with a glass of water balanced on his head, without spilling a drop.

251 Practice your waggle.

252 Pay attention to the details. You will be surprised how you imperceptibly alter your grip, weight distribution, and ball position over time. What will begin to feel right will be wrong.

253 A good followthrough is proof of the quality of the swing that went before.

254 You hit the ball farther more frequently when you don't try to hit it far.

[SAM SNEAD]

255 Try to finish with the club shaft resting on your collar.

256 Hold the finish as long as the ball is in flight.

257 **Make up your mind to strive for accuracy rather than distance in playing iron shots. If you have the slightest doubt that the club you have chosen is too short, then choose the longer one. It is a mistake to try to overhit your irons.**

[PATTY BERG]

258 Keep your head slightly behind the ball.

259 **It is not the movement of looking up that destroys good contact, but the lateral movement of the head toward the target at or before impact.**

260 To get the correct idea of the pivot and turn, imagine you are standing in a barrel up to your hips and you must complete the swing without touching the rim.

261 One reason to waggle at address is to keep moving and avoid swinging from a static start.

262 To improve the smoothness and slowness of your takeaway, imagine that the clubhead is attached to a ball and chain and you have to drag this heavy weight away from the ball.

263 To avoid freezing over the ball, try to incorporate a swing "trigger" into your pre-shot routine—Gary Player uses a slight forward press of his wrists, Jack Nicklaus swivels his chin slightly to the right.

264 **Gary Player reminded himself not to swing too fast by writing "slow" on the top of his golf glove.**

265 To improve tempo, try to build a pause into your swing at the top but only do this in practice.

266 Learn to dance! The rhythmic movements of dancing can seriously improve your footwork for golf.

267 **When driving off the tee, the ball should be placed opposite the front foot's heel.**

268 The most important single move in establishing your tempo and rhythm is your takeaway. It sets the beat for everything that comes later. Strive on every shot to move the club back as deliberately as possible.

[JACK NICKLAUS]

269 When driving, grip it extra light.

270 Grip the driver like it was a small bird.

271 The fuller the finish, the longer the ball.

272 A long drive is a product of good timing, weight shift, balance, and flexibility.

273 A properly teed-up golf ball stands with half of its body above the club head.

274 Forward slant the tee in the ground a little; this gives you a feeling of sweeping the ball away.

275 **When driving, feel your weight shift more on your rear foot on the back swing—about 90 percent back foot to 10 percent front foot.**

276 A driver has the same swing tempo as a pitching wedge.

277 Keep your swing tempo at a constant pace and you will become more consistent.

278 When playing a fairway wood, think of swinging the clubhead wide.

279 **Tee 'em high and watch 'em fly.**

280 **Tee 'em low to control where they go.**

281 With irons at address, forward press the hands so they are in front of the ball.

282 Many shots are spoiled at the last instant by efforts to add a few more yards. This impedes, rather than aids, the stroke.

[BOBBY JONES]

THE SHORT GAME

283 You can recover from a poor distance shot, but a poor chip or pitch is usually a shot lost to par.

[DAVE PELZ]

284 **One of the most important distances in golf is a circle six feet in diameter around the hole—statistics prove that you will make most of your putts from within that length.**

285 Consider this: You hit a perfect drive and a really good second and are on the green 45 feet from the hole. The slightest error on your putt and you are struggling to make par. Meanwhile, your opponent hits his ball in the rough, hacks to thirty yards, and then pitches to within three feet. Your perfect shot was the drive; his was the pitch. He wins the hole.

286 If you hit six greens, you've missed twelve. Remember: After putting, chipping and pitching are more important than any other shot.

287 To chip well, aim to hit a spot. Check the variables and decide what shot to hit. Then pick a spot for the ball to land and visualize the ball landing there and running to the hole.

[JOHNNY MILLER]

288 How to set up for the perfect chip: Place the clubface standing square to the target, feet together. Turn the toes toward the target so the ball is positioned backward in your stance, opposite the right heel. Lightly grip down on the shaft with hands ahead of the ball. Keep weight on the left foot.

289 How to play the perfect chip: Set up as above, then swing the club mainly with the forearms, using the shoulders. The right shoulder should feel as though it is moving vertically upward on the backstroke and downward on the swing.
You want to have the feeling of the club striking downward. Always keep the hands ahead of the ball.

290 To get a chip to go over an obstacle, try a 60-degree lob wedge. Don't use a sand wedge because the large flange—curved area that protrudes from the sole—will impede good contact, especially off bare lies.

291 **The commonest error is taking the club back too far and decelerating on impact.**

[TOM WATSON]

292 How to play a pitch shot 20 to 100 yards from the hole: Position the ball about three inches inside the left foot. Angle the feet toward the target. Push the hands forward to keep them ahead of the ball. Swing as if for a full shot but stop it half way. This shot involves the body and the arms.

293 The short game comprises 70 percent of all golf shots played.

294 Take lessons from a pro to master the short game. The intricacies of chipping and putting are difficult to grasp and no amount of book reading can replace practical teaching.

295 If you are a beginner, start by learning putting and chipping—this is how many of the world's best players started.

296 **To help develop hand-eye coordination and to improve judgment and distance control take a few practice swings while looking at the target.**

297 Allow the loft of the club to dictate how far the ball will go rather than swing length.

298 Keep wrists locked when chipping and use a pendulum motion on the backswing.

299 How to play the up and over chip: Position the ball in the middle of your stance. Keep feet close together and stand with shoulders slightly open to the target. Swing with some leg action, transferring your weight from back to front during the swing. Keep your hands ahead of the ball and strike downward at the back of the ball. Keep your head down until after the ball has gone.

300 The younger you start, the more you should focus on the short game. It is hard to have a perfect swing when you are still growing. But the touch you develop by working on your short game will stick with you forever.

[BOB ESTES]

301 **When chipping remember: Fewer moving parts means more reliability.**

302 Make quarter, half, and three-quarter swings with your wedges and note how far the ball travels with each one—you then have three different length shots with each club.

303 There is no quicker way to lower your handicap than the ability to consistently chip close enough for one putt instead of two.

[GARY PLAYER]

304 Swing length determines the speed of the clubhead, not the wrists.

305 Try to keep the strong muscles of the forearms, wrists, and hands out of your short game as much as possible.

306 A key to chipping success is to create a straight line with the left arm and the shaft at address and keep that relationship throughout the shot.

307 Getting the ball out of a greenside sand trap is easy when you know these rules: Use a sand wedge with a large sole. Grip the club lightly, striking the sand behind the ball. Swing through to a full finish.

308 To ensure you hit behind and under the ball in a sand trap, play the ball forward in your stance.

309 To create a descending blow and low running trajectory on a chip shot, play the ball back in the stance.

310 For pitch and wedge shots to the green, play the ball in the center of the stance.

311 In sand traps, the better the lie, the farther forward you should position the ball in your stance—this will ensure the clubhead hits the sand before the ball, creating extra control.

312 Test the sand for depth by planting your feet firmly in it.

313 Bad lie in the sand? Keep the ball back in your stance—this will ensure the clubhead makes contact with the ball at its most powerful point, forcing the ball out of the sand trap.

314 Try putting from the sand if the ball is lying on firm, dry, level sand and there is virtually no lip.

315 Try chipping from a sand trap if there is only a slight lip—play the ball off the toe of the club to reduce backspin.

316 If you chip from the sand, make sure that most of your weight is on the left foot.

317 In dry sand, try to take more of it.

318 In wet sand, use a pitching wedge and square the clubface—this will help you hit the ball cleanly.

319 If you have an uphill lie in a sand trap, take less sand.

320 If you have a good lie in a sand trap, try to spank the sand to get the ball out quickly and with spin.

321 One of the best ways to shave shots off your game is to spend some time in the sand.

[GREG NORMAN]

322 **A plugged ball in a sand trap? You need to get behind and underneath it—imagine you want to shovel it out.**

323 **Invest in a sand wedge with good bounce—a big flange prevents the clubhead from getting buried in the sand.**

324 Sand shots are played with the left hand—slightly tighten your grip with the left hand and loosen the right.

325 **A downhill lie in a sand trap? The ball is going to fly out low, so release the clubhead down the slope and chase the ball with the clubhead toward the target.**

326 In the sand, the farther forward your ball is positioned, the more you should open the clubface.

327 The farther back the ball is positioned in your stance when in a sand trap, the more you should close the clubface.

328 The more you closed the clubface of a wedge, the more square you must aim.

329 With pitches and sand shots, the more open the clubface, the farther left you should aim.

330 To ensure consistency of distance, complete your follow through when pitching or chipping.

331 A drive is nearly always a drive, but a chip may be anything and is rarely the same thing twice.

[BOBBY JONES]

332 **If you don't hit through the ball with your sand wedge, you risk leaving the ball in the trap.**

333 **A key to successful sand play is to allow your arms and shoulders to relax.**

334 The key to bravado is practice. I've practiced every bunker lie there is and can call on that memory to think my way out of trouble every time.

[GARY PLAYER]

335 Avoid using the sand wedge on bare tight lies—the sole will bounce and cause a thin.

336 Avoid hitting into slopes on approach shots. Aim for a flat area of the green where the bounce is easier to predict.

337 Try using a three wood from fluffy greenside grass. It will give extra lift and is more effective than a putter. Hold the club on the shaft below the grip and swing as if chipping.

338 Chip shots should be on the ground and rolling as soon as possible—to practice, try chipping under a bench.

339 From thick rough, try using a sand wedge—the curved sole will cause the clubhead to bounce and avoid a fat shot.

340 Chip swings should be smooth, easy, and of uniform speed regardless of the distance required. Let the swing length, club loft, and shaft length dictate the distance—not the force of the shot.

341 Use a variety of clubs around the green: For a long shot covering a lot of green, you might use a middle iron. For a mid-range chip, try a seven, eight, or nine iron. For a short chip, try a wedge. Change the loft, not the swing.

342 **For fringe, uphill, and longer chip shots, try using a six, seven, or eight iron. Keep wrists and arms locked and swing as if putting.**

343 When using a long iron from the edge of a green, keep your hands ahead of the clubhead and ensure that your followthrough is the same length or longer than your backswing.

344 To control your half wedge, limit your backswing to the nine o'clock position.

345 To improve your stability when chipping, hit a few practice chips with your right foot off the ground.

346 **Always putt from off the green if possible. Putts are generally more consistent than chip shots.**

347 Around the green, wherever possible play the club that keeps the ball nearest to the ground. Putt rather than chip, chip rather than pitch.

[BILLY CASPER]

348 **Basic rules for getting out of sand traps: Open your stance with the ball in the center and hit about two inches behind the ball with a smooth, continuous swing.**

349 The pop shot is ideal if you need to hit over an object and land soft on the green: Position the ball a little forward in your stance, open the clubface, and, even though the landing area is close, take a full swing. The blade should hit an inch or so behind the ball with a wrist popping motion. This makes the clubface lead the hands, and the ball will pop up quickly and land softly with very little roll.

350 If your ball is buried in the sand, use a pitching wedge and play the ball back in your stance. Close the clubface a little and hit an inch or two behind the ball. You must complete the followthrough.

351 **For a powerful blast out of a trap, strike the sand two to four inches behind the ball.**

352 To get the ball up quickly from under the lip of a trap, start the backswing by cocking your wrists upward first and then continue with your normal backswing. The downswing is the same as normal, but you must release the wrists before impact. This steep cut through the sand will pop the ball up quickly and softly.

353 A light grip gives extra feel.

354 Aim your pitches and chips onto the heart of the green if possible. The putting surface has a more predictable bounce than the fairway.

355 Take your wrists out of the chip shot—think dead hands.

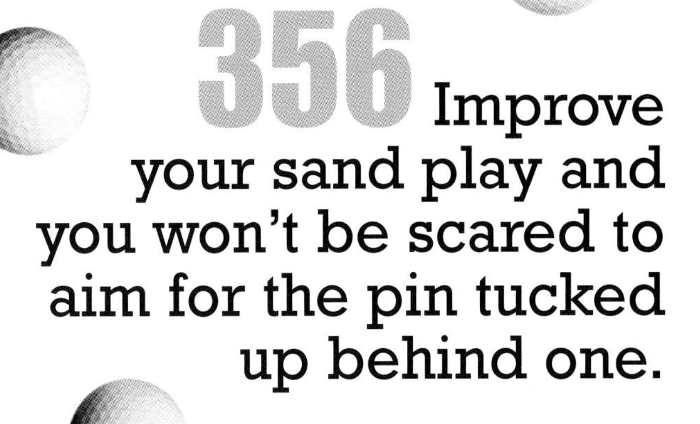

356 Improve your sand play and you won't be scared to aim for the pin tucked up behind one.

357 Sand traps should not be feared—pros prefer being in a trap than greenside rough.

358 Keep the clubface open in soft sand. Imagine a glass balanced on the face throughout the shot.

[BEN CRENSHAW]

359 **Improve posture when chipping and pitching. Remember to maintain that "tail up" feeling in your lower back.**

360 The best teachers often give two basic lessons for good chipping: Keep most of your weight on your left leg and get your hands ahead of the ball in order to strike down on it and get good, crisp contact.

361 Perfect your technique before developing touch and feel.

362 Think "wristy risky" from 20 yards in—don't use your wrists, just turn your shoulders.

363 Practice chipping from a variety of lies and grass lengths.

364 Study the lie and grass length before deciding on club and shot type.

365 From 40 yards in, aim to hole it!

366 Visualize your chip shot while making practice swings: Pick a landing area on the green from which the ball will roll up to the hole. Choose the loft necessary to do this and then take a few practice swings while focusing on the landing area.

367

Practice chipping from the very edge of the green and don't give up until three consecutive shots finish within three feet of the hole and one goes in.

368 When chipping on downhill lies, keep your weight on your left side throughout the swing and the clubface as near to the surface of the grass as possible.

369 Gripping low on the club gives more control but remember to move slightly closer to the ball to maintain your spine angle. Slumping your posture will lead to a sloppy shot.

370 From just off the green, practice getting the ball to the hole with one specific club and then stick to it on the course.

371 Using a golf cart can compromise your chances of success by restricting your club selection possibilities. Take a variety of clubs to the ball so you have a selection to choose from rather than risk hitting with the wrong club.

372 Putting from off the green not an option? Then try the putt-chip technique—hold an eight iron like a putter and swing as if putting.

373 To roll the ball long distances with greater accuracy and distance, try the chip-putt technique. Use a putter and swing it as if chipping.

374 Always accelerate through the shots.

375 **Keep hands well ahead of the ball when playing from a bare lie to ensure crisp contact.**

376 To check your stance is ahead of the ball, hang a club vertically from your shirt buttons when addressing the ball as normal. The clubhead should be in front of the spot where the ball lies.

377 **Lee Trevino uses a four iron for long chips because he believes the extra roll it creates is more consistent than a chip shot.**

378 The ball is 50 feet from a flat green: A ball hit with a four iron will spend less than five feet in the air and 45 feet on the ground. With a seven iron, it will spend about 10 in the air and 40 on the ground, while with a wedge, it will spend 30 in the air and 20 on the ground. Judging carry is harder to judge than roll, so if you have the option, the chip and run is always the safest shot.

379 Pros spend most their practice sessions on the short game.

380 **Remember that once the ball hits the green and starts to roll, it behaves just like a putt. Before chipping or pitching read the green just as you would for a putt to gauge the path to the hole.**

381 To improve feel, try throwing balls at a target and watching how they react when they hit the ground.

382 Decide on the type of chip you are going to hit and then stick to it. Either focus on the end target and aim to stop the ball by the hole or pick a specific landing area and run the ball up to the hole.

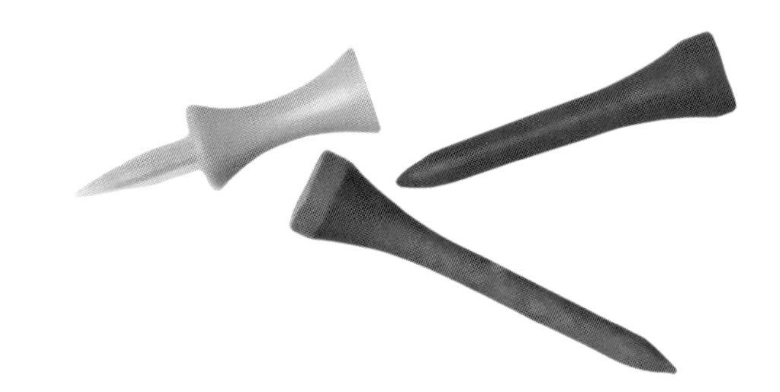

383 Don't show off!

The long lob shot might look spectacular but is difficult to judge. Don't use it until you have to.

384 Don't "scoop"the ball when chipping. Remember to keep your weight on the front foot and hands ahead of the ball.

385 Take more practice shots the nearer you get to the hole.

386

Are you a cricketer? The feel for a chip is very similar to the forward defense stroke at the crease.

387

The worse the lie, the more important to hit the ball on the downswing.

[LEE TREVINO]

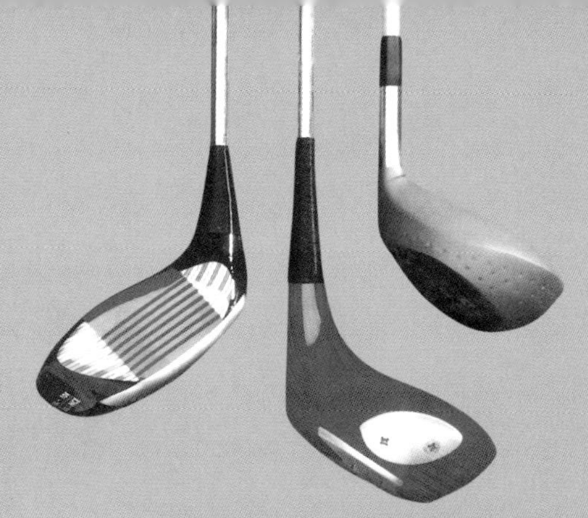

388 When does a chip become a pitch? The answer is when the backswing is long enough to require a hinge of the wrists.

389 A good steep downswing is required when chipping. To practice: Lay your umbrella on the ground parallel with your feet, three inches behind the ball. If you catch it on the way down your swing is too shallow.

390 Under pressure around the green, always go to the straightest blade that will do the job. It may require a three iron to get the roll you need.

[HARVEY PENICK]

391 **If the lie is bare, it is a good idea to increase the speed of the swing slightly in order to ensure a crisp contact should the club hit the ground first.**

392 If you choose the target area method of judging a chip, pick the smallest target you can.

393 Is the ground between you and the green too rough to putt across? Then it is most likely too rough to bounce a ball on with any predictability, so choose a shot that will land the ball on the green. This avoids a poor bounce from ruining your efforts.

394 Uphill lies accentuate loft, so when chipping, choose a less lofted club.

395 **Putt if you can, chip if you can't putt, and pitch when you can't chip.**

396 Better to leave a chip short on an uphill slope than to risk a tricky downhill putt.

397 **Always check your alignment. First be precise on how you set the clubface behind the ball and allow it to dictate your stance.**

398 A weak grip is essential for a good chipping and pitching. Ensure you can only see one knuckle of the left hand when looking down at your grip as you address the ball. This will increase your sensitivity, reduce the tendency to break the wrists, and help prevent stubbing the clubhead into the ground behind the ball.

399 To control distance and vary it, experiment with shortening the shaft by gripping down the club. Watch how the same strength shot with different length shafts will produce a different length shot.

400 Don't grip the club too hard. Although the best chip swing is the one in which the wrists play no active part, remember not to be too rigid in the wrists. Pros have what they call "light hands."

401 In deep rough beside the green? The best solution is to play the shot as though you were in the sand. Open the face, open your stance, and take a good swing at the ball, aiming to slice through the grass about two inches behind it. Make sure you followthrough.

402 Prevent quitting on a chip—practice making your followthrough longer than your backswing and always hold the finish.

403 There are three ways to take distance off an iron to the green: Grip down the club, shorten the backswing, and shorten the throughswing. Try these on the practice ground with an eight iron, both separately and in combination, and study the differences in flight and stopping distance they produce.

404 A good practice drill is to take three balls and try to get down in two with all three from various distances.

405 In his heyday Ben Hogan hit more greens than any player in history yet he would practice short shots from off the green for hours on end, day after day. Isn't that interesting—and educational?

[LEE TREVINO]

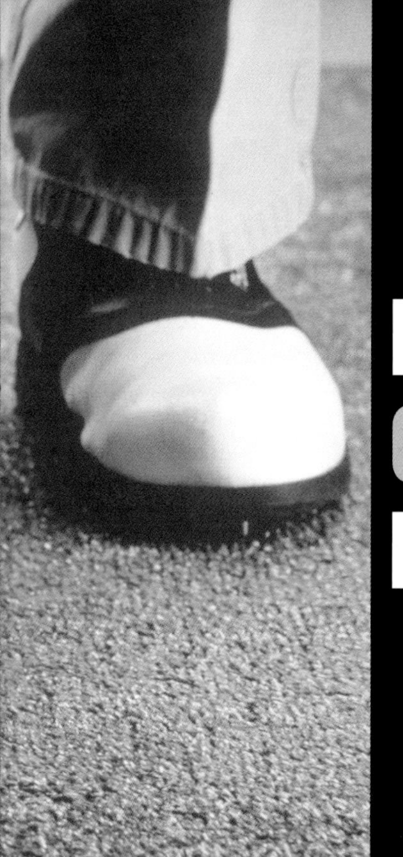

PUTTING CAN BE FUN

406 **Putting—a game within a game—might justly be said to be the most important of golf.**

[BOBBY JONES]

407 The first fundamental of putting is to take the putter straight back and through the target line, keeping the putter face square.

408 Stand square to your aim line. During practice, place a club on the ground, aiming toward the hole; stand parallel to the club and putt along that line.

409 **The most common way to grip a putter is the reverse overlap—keep all the fingers of the right hand on the shaft while the left forefinger rests over the last three fingers of the right.**

410 Don't collapse the left wrist at impact—you will pull it and the ball will go straight left.

411 There are many practice aids available that can help you to keep the putterface square to the line at impact. Any one of them is a good cheap investment—but you must resolve to persevere and use it. Results do not come instantly.

412 Always putt to make it.

[BRAD FAXON]

413 Develop a putting routine and stick to it.

414 Note the general slope of the green as you approach it.

415 Watch your playing partners' putts to get an idea of the general speed of the green.

416 Study the line from behind the hole and behind the ball.

417 Even professionals miss half of their six-foot putts.

[DAVE PELZ]

418 If you are missing three-footers, concentrate on the feeling of the putt rather than the target.

419 **Get over the fear of short putts—don't freeze over the ball; choose your line and hit confidently.**

420 **Choose a line and choose a target to aim at between you and the hole—this will help with accuracy, especially on long putts.**

421 Commit to the line of your putt.

422 To gauge speed, make a couple of practice strokes standing behind the ball and looking down the line of the putt.

423 To prepare for the putt, set up slightly away from the ball and make two or three practice swings.

424 **Imagine your last practice swing is exactly how you want to make the putt.**

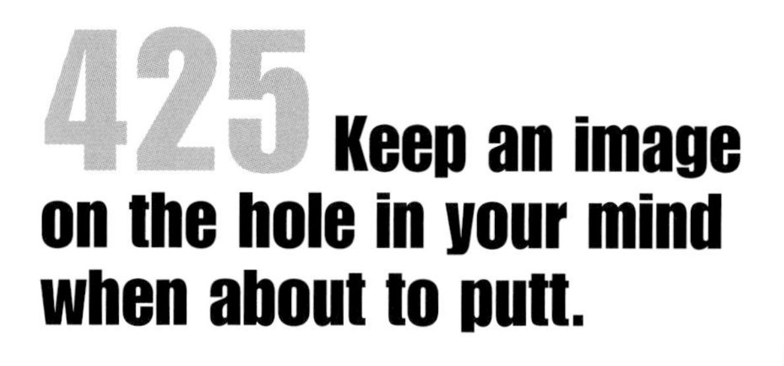

425 Keep an image on the hole in your mind when about to putt.

426 Once settled over the ball, take a last glance at the target and just let the putt go.

427 There are no points for style when it comes to putting. It's getting the ball in the cup that counts.

[BRIAN SWARBRICK]

428 Practice putting 40 percent of the time—40 percent of strokes made on the course are putts.

429 Putting well boosts confidence in every other part of the game.

430 Don't have a sense of dread when walking onto the green.

431 **Will yourself to want to make the putt.**

432 In putting, the inability to forget is infinitely more devastating than the inability to remember.

[DR. BOB ROTELLA]

433 Putting is an acquired taste; you can learn to love it.

434 If you start to tell yourself that you cannot putt, you can bet your bottom peso that you won't get the ball in the hole from three feet.

[LEE TREVINO]

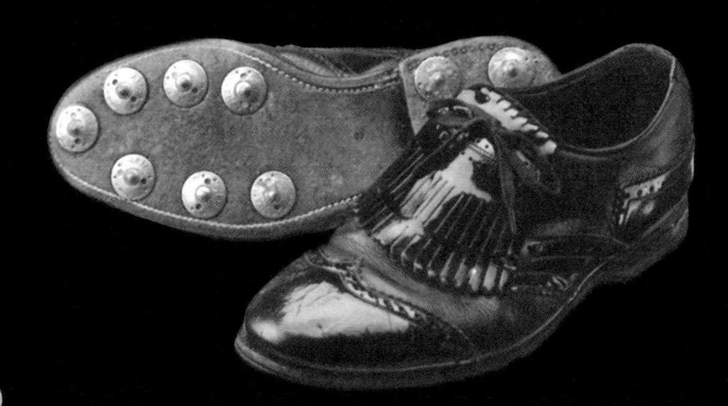

435 Get used to the feel of one brand of golf ball and stick to it.

436 Practice reading the greens on your home course.

437 Grip the putter lightly, as though you were squeezing an egg.

438 On long putts, choose a spot along the line of the putt between you and the hole but in range of your peripheral view. Aim to roll the ball over that spot.

439 **Holes become crowned over time, causing putts to veer off. Make sure your putts are firm enough to hold the line.**

440 **The optimum speed for a putt is 17 inches past the hole. This is fast enough for it to hold the line and slow enough not to lip out.**

[DAVE PELZ]

441 Even putting on a crazy golf course will help you develop feel!

442 Swing the putter like a pendulum from the shoulders, not the wrists.

443 **Allow the length of swing to dictate the speed of the putt.**

444 Never give a putt that beats you.

[HARRY VARDON]

445 Make the followthrough slightly longer than the backswing to ensure that the putterface accelerates through impact.

446 Hold the finish until the ball drops.

447 Good putting is a combination of three ingredients: a proper stroke, sound judgment, and confidence.

[CRAIG STADLER]

448 Always clean the blade of your putter before making the putt.

449 To help your focus when putting, concentrate on the ball's number, logo, or one of the dimples.

450 Set up is crucial when putting.

451 The ball should be directly under your left eye when putting.

452 To check the ball position, try dangling your putter from the bridge of your nose. It should point to just behind the ball.

453 Keep the V-shape formed by the hands and arms constant throughout the putt.

454 To produce a weaker hit on downhill putts, try putting with the ball nearer to the toe of the putter.

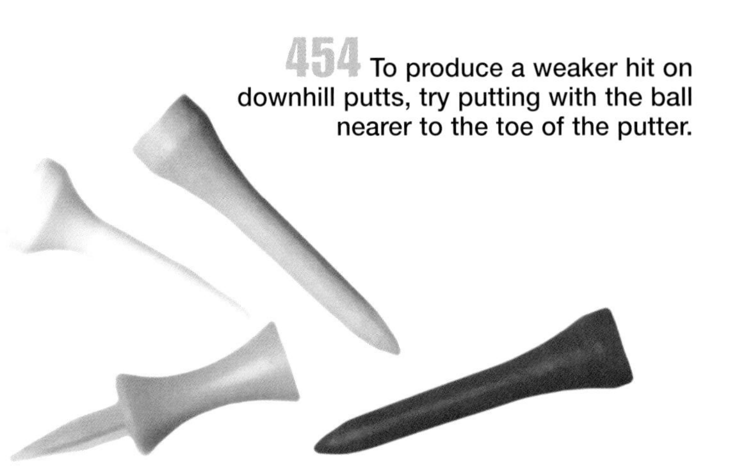

455 To help you aim, replace your ball on the green with the name logo in line with the line of your putt and then putt through the logo line.

456 Practicing short putts does not always help the yips.

457 **Golfers who don't care never get the yips.**

[DAVE PELZ]

458 The main way to cure the yips is to forget the last putt you missed.

459 **If you take the kids to a crazy golf course, take your own putter along so you can get used to the feel of it under all kinds of situations.**

460 The only club in the bag specifically designed to get the ball into the cup is the putter. Why not learn to use it first?

[JACKIE BURKE, JR.]

461 **Concentrate on rhythm when putting.**

462 The golfer who wins always putts well.

463 **The one thing I never change is my belief that I am going to regain my touch.**

[ARNOLD PALMER]

464 It is easier to stroke a 12-foot putt than a three-foot putt because we don't fear missing from 12 feet.

465 **The secret to holing short putts is to commit to the line and stroke it firmly.**

466 Check for grain by running your putterhead across the surface of the green. It will snag up against the grain. But only do this in practice. During play it is illegal.

467 Take note of the grain. Is the grass growing against the direction you want the ball to travel? If it is, it could shorten your shot by 50 percent.

468 Listen for the putts to drop; you don't gain anything by looking up after it.

[TIGER WOODS]

469 **When the green reflects the sun, it appears brighter as you are looking down the grain.**

470 If the grain is in the direction of the cross slope, the putt will break more than normal.

471 Uphill putts against the grain will be slow.

472 Good putters believe they are good putters.

[RAYMOND FLOYD]

473 With long putts, speed is more important than break.

474 **On short putts never aim outside the hole unless the break is severe.**

475 Aim for a spot along the line of the putt and make the putterhead hit through toward it.

476 To calm the nerves on short putts, try lengthening the backswing slightly.

477 The thing that hurt my putting most was thinking too much about how I was making the stroke and not enough about getting the ball into the hole.

[BOBBY JONES]

478 If you are missing a lot of three-footers, check your alignment and your stroke. If these are okay, think about gripping the putter a little more lightly.

479 **Before a round, hole 20 consecutive three-foot putts.**

480 Being sound from six feet widens your target to a twelve-foot circle round the hole. You can't spend too much time practicing six-footers.

[RAYMOND FLOYD]

481 Practice aiming at a tee peg instead of a hole. If you can consistently hit a tee from three feet, you will have no trouble with a hole.

482 On long putts you are more likely to go 10 feet past the hole than 10 feet either side of it.

483 Give up control to gain control.

[DR. BOB ROTELLA]

484 On putts over 50 feet, aim to lag the ball to within three feet.

485 Consistently missing left on long putts means you are probably collapsing the left wrist.

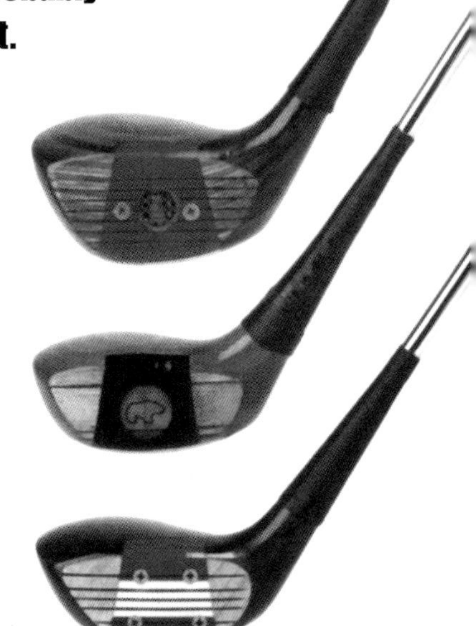

486 It pays not to practice long putts too much. The time is better spent holing putts from 15 feet and fewer.

487 Taking the high road—playing more break instead of less—makes sense. A ball is more likely to fall down into the hole from the high side. It also encourages rolling the ball at a slower speed, meaning it is less likely to run too far past the hole should it miss.

[DAVE PELZ]

488 Your worst putt will be better than your best chip.

489 Putt from off the green unless the grain is against you, the terrain is bumpy, you have a poor lie, or the fringe is long.

490 Thinking the way you have always thought will almost certainly assure you putt the way you always have.

[DR. BOB ROTELLA]

491 When practicing putting, stand to the ball with an "invisible" putter in your hands and picture yourself making the putt—then take hold of the putter and do it for real.

492 **The smaller the putting target, the better.**

493 Don't let anger get in the way of focus—if you miss a bad putt, don't miss the next.

494 Get your putter fitted to your stroke—if you grip down the club have it shortened.

495 Long putters and belly putters work for the pros. So try them.

496 **All good putters have good rhythm. Study the pros.**

497 Rhythm and repetition help to clear your mind while stroking the putt.

498 **Almost all putts break slightly but the question is whether the break will be enough to miss the hole—don't over-exaggerate the angle.**

499 To keep your putterface square and ensure you take the club back straight, try this practice drill. Connect two meat skewers together with a 12-foot piece of string. Stick the skewers into the ground so the string is tight and then stand square to it, somewhere at its midpoint. Place the ball directly under the string and take your putter back, keeping it in line with the string.

500 When reading breaks, remember that the ball has to start out wider than the widest point of the arc to make the hole.

501 Once the putter is aimed at the target, keep your eyes and shoulders parallel to that line.

502 **Be relaxed at address—if you are uneasy you will not make a good stroke.**

503 Get a friend to check your alignment.

504 Eliminate body movement by imagining you are set in concrete up to your hips.

505 To keep the putterface square, feel as if your right palm is pushing toward the hole.

506 Practice hitting the sweet spot of your putter: Stick two pieces of plasticine onto either side of the face, just wider than the golf ball. If you hit the ball slightly off center, it will be deflected by the plasticine.

507 Keep your hands high and away from the body when putting.

508 Essentially the putter is an extension of your left hand so always carry it with your left hand.

[HARVEY PENICK]

509 **Keep the putter low to the ground throughout the stroke.**

510 **A good putting posture allows the arms to hang freely and vertically.**

511 Focus your mind—make a couple of practice putts while looking at the hole.

512 **To aid stability, place a little more weight on the front foot.**

513 Always have the flag attended on long putts because the flagstick aids perception of distance and green reading.

514 Generally, greens get slower as the day progresses, unless it is a hot day.

515 If in doubt, aim for the hole.

516 Check a putt from all sides to help you judge the distance and any undulations in the path.

517 When reading a line, your first impression is often the best.

518 If a putt looks straight, don't stare at it too long because you will invent a break that isn't there.

[CORY PAVIN]

519 Inspect the area directly around the hole before you putt.

520 To improve feel, try removing your golf glove before putting.

521 Uphill putts have less break.

522 To help read the line of a putt, stand well back, or, if you can, below the level of the green.

523 It is not physically possible to make the little ball travel over uncertain ground for three or four feet with any degree of regularity.

[WALTER HAGEN]

524 Pace out a long putt. It is better to know exactly how far it is than to guess.

525 Practice putting wherever you can—the bedroom, hotel, and office carpets are perfect.

526 To read a line, look at your ball from behind the hole. Imagine it running toward you. How far would it roll to the left or right? That is the difference you must allow.

527 **The forefinger and thumb of the right hand give the most feel on putts.**

528 Always observe the surface of the green carefully, clean your line of sand and debris and repair pitch marks, but remember you cannot repair spike marks.

529 Make your practice swing parallel to the putting line—this helps to focus your mind on what's ahead.

530 To help master long putts, practice putting balls from one fringe of the practice green to the other. When you judge it perfectly, note the length of your backswing and pace of the putt—you now know exactly how to hit a putt that distance.

531 The chief reaction among amateurs to poor putting is exasperation, combined with a sort of vague hope that it will get better by some miracle.

[JACK NICKLAUS]

532 Once you have practiced the stroke, trust your body to make the putt.

533 You will have a favorite putt. Practice the ones you don't like.

534 Keep your head down when putting—focus on a blade of grass behind the ball on short putts and keep your gaze on that until you hear the putt drop.

535 To improve touch and feel, practice putting without a target for a few strokes.

536 Aim at the back of the hole.

537 The overwhelming majority of unsuccessful putts are missed not because they are misjudged but because they are mishit.

[JACKIE BURKE, JR.]

538 **The man who can putt is a match for anyone.**

[WILLY PARK JR.]

539 The wind can affect your putts but remember that it blows in gusts rather than constantly.

540 Your muscles can remember a movement for about eight seconds. Try to make your actual stroke no longer than eight seconds after your last practice stroke.

[DAVE PELZ]

541 The best way to improve putting is to get feedback—ask a golfing friend to watch you and give advice.

542 Warm up for the course by making a few 40-foot lag putts first. Then hit a few 15-footers. Finally, hole five six-footers and 20 three-footers consecutively without missing.

543 I putt and miss. I putt and miss. I putt and miss. I putt and it went in. —Seve Ballesteros when asked how he had four putted in a tournament.

544 Watching your putting stroke on video can help you see where you are going wrong.

545 There is no luck in putting; the good and bad even out in the end.

546 Always have a practice swing before you make a stroke.

547 To teach yourself how to cope under pressure on the course, try to give yourself tasks off the course that will mimic the type of pressure you would feel on the course.

548 **Buy a practice hole that you can use on the carpet at home and make 10 consecutive six-foot putts every morning and 10 every evening.**

KPMG
Consulting

549 **The difference between a good swinger of the club and a great player lies between the ears.**

[GARY PLAYER]

550 Relax—concentrate—have confidence.

551 Think of the shot you have to make, not the result.

552 What separates the great players from the good players, or the 15-handicap player from the 20-handicap player, is not so much ability as brainpower and mental equilibrium.

[ARNOLD PALMER]

553 **The hardest part is letting go of your thoughts—practice it.**

554 The trick of golf is the ability to try without trying.

555 Ask yourself why you play golf. If enjoyment is not one of the reasons, then there is something wrong.

556 **The game of golf is 90 percent mental; the other 10 percent is mental.**

[MULLIGAN'S LAWS]

557 Concentration is impossible without believing in your ability. Doubt destroys your game.

558 If you play not to lose rather than to win, you will most likely be defeated.

559 Refocus your thoughts. Instead of saying to yourself: "I must avoid the water," say "I want to hit this down the fairway."

560 **There is only one way to exercise your mind, use it.**

[GARY PLAYER]

561 In golf, things invariably get worse before they get better.

562 Fear of failure weakens the will and usually leads to that which we fear most.

563 Focus by choosing a specific swing thought and concentrate on that for the next three holes.

564 Trust in your ability can only be built through practice.

565 Golf is not a game of perfect it is a game of confidence.

[DR. BOB ROTELLA]

566 When in trouble accept that the worse the lie, the greater the sacrifice you will have to make.

567 **In a troublesome lie, think good contact before all else to avoid choosing the wrong club.**

568 Tension and anxiety cause more misses than a lack of care.

[BOBBY JONES]

569 If you don't think you can do it, you most likely won't.

570 After each game, remember the best three putts you holed.

571 **After you get the basics down, it's all mental.**

[KEN VENTURI]

572 If you can make a shot once, you can do it again.

573 Competitive golf is played mainly on a five-and-a-half-inch course, the space between your ears.

[BOBBY JONES]

574 **Think big to be big—poor self-perception is the enemy of progress.**

575 Positive thinking creates positive outcomes.

576 Success depends on your attitude and skill at the short game.

577 It takes so long to realize that you can't always replicate your swing. The only thing you can control is your attitude toward your next shot.

[MARK MCCUMBER]

578 Before you go to sleep, imagine you are playing a round at your local course and remember, one stroke at a time, the best way to play each hole. See how many holes you can go before losing concentration—it certainly beats counting sheep!

579 To relax between shots, try humming a tune to yourself.

580 Shrug off failure quickly—choose not to be angry with yourself.

581 **Take care with your body language—when you are down, your shoulders will sag and this will worsen your stroke-making ability. Think always of trying to maintain an upright, confident gait.**

582 To be good at golf you need desire to do well, determination to work hard, and diligence to keep going through the bad times.

583 Faith in your ability and feel for the shot go hand in hand. You don't get one without the other.

584 Improvement requires a persistent attitude toward practice and the patience to wait for the rewards.

585 **Anger with oneself achieves nothing.**

586 If you are playing well, remember you are the one doing it.

587 Composure in difficulties helps you concentrate. And with concentration comes the confidence to improve.

588 Train yourself to have a good technique, but trust yourself to hit the shots.

589 More bad shots come from poor thinking than poor technique.

590 Before playing a shot, pick a target as small as you can and keep focused on it.

591 **Stay in the present—think about the shot at hand, not the score.**

592 Develop a consistent pre-shot routine. Look at your target, look at your ball, and just let the swing go.

593 You may not always hit a good shot if you think you will, but you rarely hit a good shot if you think you won't.

594 Don't think about swing mechanics during the shot.

595 There are no instant fixes in sports psychology. You have to practice mental skills as much as physical ones.

596 Your best golf is an indication of your ability, not a quirk of good fortune.

597 Be decisive. If a doubt creeps into your mind, stop and refocus on the shot.

598 Keep telling yourself you are a good golfer.

599 See how many holes you can play without dropping shots and carry them over from one round to the next.

600 **If you can make two pars in a row there is no reason why you cannot make three, four, or eighteen.**

601 Think to yourself: I must keep my muscles and shoulders relaxed.

602 Even the best golfers make mistakes.

603 On the first tee, a golfer must expect only two things of himself: to have fun and to focus his mind properly on every shot.

[DR. BOB ROTELLA]

604 Golf is game of mistake elimination.

605 It is never too late to start making pars.

606 **See each shot as a challenge. Set yourself a realistic goal for each and achieve it.**

607 Complaining about a bad lie or a poor position will curb your success and ruin your enjoyment.

608 You cannot achieve any goal if you have negative thoughts in your mind.

[GARY PLAYER]

609 Be patient—practice will produce results when you least expect it.

610 Monitor your thoughts to stop them slipping into negativity.

611 **Don't allow yourself to dislike anyone in your club. You may have to play with them one day and it will affect your game more than theirs.**

612 Quality is better than quantity. A well-struck 200-yard three wood down the fairway is better than a 250-yard driver into the woods.

613 **To do the best you can, you need to combine your physical ability with smart thinking.**

614 Losers never admit that failure is their own fault. Winners always do because they are happy to take the blame for success.

615 **Feeling fear is normal. It is impossible not to have it and courage is required to face it.**

616 The champion only reigns until the next competition. You will have another chance—so prepare for it!

617 On the course, adopt the attitude of champions. Off the course, adopt the demeanor of a club member.

618 **You learn golf all the time, you can't learn it all at once.**

[DAVIS LOVE, JR.]

619 After each round, remember how many good shots you had and try to beat that number in the next round.

620 Correct golf is not like riding a bicycle, it can be forgotten.

621 When I hit a shot into trouble, I usually expect the worst. When I get there and find I can actually hit the ball—it changes my mood for the better.

[CORY PAVIN]

622 The only way to get used to pressure is to feel it, so play in competitions and take the time to lose before you learn how to win.

623 Watch your playing partner's shots and learn from them.

624 Experience counts. You cannot become a good golfer without it.

625 Relax on the course—get serious in practice.

626 Record all the details of your round: your shots, your putts, the number of fairways hit off the tee, the greens hit in regulation, and the times you missed the green. This will help you to see your weaknesses and what you need to practice.

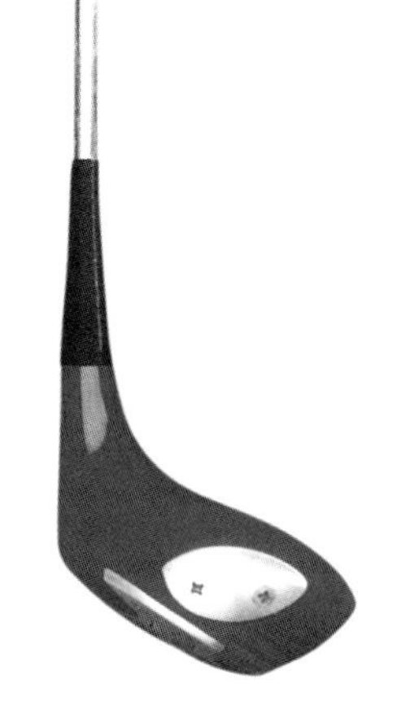

627 Trouble? What trouble?

[TIGER WOODS]

628 To help your focus, build an image of the perfect shot by running through a pre-shot checklist. One: Pick a target. Two: Study the terrain. Three: Check the wind strength and direction. Four: Check your lie. Five: Check your stance. Six: Imagine the flight path the ball is going to take to hit the target.

629 **Top players know they will eventually play well if they keep a positive attitude.**

630 A routine is not a routine if you have to think about it.

[DAVIS LOVE III]

631 Be disciplined in shot selection—don't waste shots by trying the impossible.

632 Training your mind to visualize the shot takes as long as it does to train your body to physically hit it.

633 **Forget the last shot. Good or bad, it won't help you make the next.**

634 In golf, once you can play a little, the key to success is confidence.

[GAY BREWER]

635 Talking about how bad you are is easier than talking about how good you are because nobody wants to appear conceited. But negativity eats away at your confidence—don't do it.

636 Tell yourself every day that you always make three birdies on every round.

637 While walking to your ball, rest your mind a little from the game. Focus on the shot when you reach it.

638 **A game of golf lasts for four hours and you can only concentrate for 40 minutes at a time, so accept that you will have momentary lapses.**

639 The brain cannot differentiate between do and don't commands, so if your last thought before swinging is, "Don't hit it in the lake," more likely than not, it will go in the lake.

640 **If you've played the shot in practice you can play it on the course.**

[DAVIS LOVE III]

641 If you hit a good drive, remember that you must still strive to make the next shot as good as it can possibly be. There are no easy shots in golf.

642 If you have to think about swing mechanics, take two practice swings. On the first, think about the mechanics, on the second, just swing.

643 Commit yourself to a shot—trying to steer the ball never works.

644 To stay focused, some players put elastic bands around their wrists to literally snap themselves awake before every shot.

645 Sam Snead used to relate to the golf ball as if it were human. He would talk to it and try to charm it into his confidence—sometimes he even felt the ball was reciprocating.

646 Don't overreact to bad shots—just accept them.

647 Focus on where you want to hit the ball, not where you don't.

648 Don't get into the habit of thinking that poor play is a true reflection of your character or ability. It is just poor play and you will begin to play well again—be sure of that!

649 Golf is what we do for fun—so have fun.

650 If in doubt about your club, make a positive decision to hit the shot as well as you can. If the club was wrong, you will not be far off target, but if you have doubt in your mind as you make the shot, you will probably get into trouble.

651 **Build up a bank of good memories and don't dwell on disasters.**

652 No one is cursed by voodoo. There is no lid on the hole for anyone.

[JOHN DALY]

653 Good players say that when they play well, they end a round without any idea of how many shots they have played. This is the ideal mental state for playing great golf.

654 Hypnosis works—buy a book that teaches you techniques of self-hypnosis.

655 Carry around cue cards of positive thoughts for inspiration. Reading a phrase such as, "I will play better if I relax and have fun" over and over between rounds will eventually seep into the subconscious and influence your game.

656 If you hit a good shot, tell yourself so.

657 If you are distracted while taking a shot, refocus your mind by thoroughly running through your pre-shot routine.

658 If you feel like you are rushing, you are probably over-anxious or too pumped up. Breathe deeply, relax, and consciously direct the will to walk slowly and slow down your practice swings.

659 **Try talking to yourself to dampen down anxiety. Repeat to yourself: "relax, relax, relax" and breathe deeply.**

660 **Concentration lapses often occur because you are placing too much emphasis on technique and mechanics. Prevent this by repeating a mood word or phrase such as "easy" or "let it go" before swinging.**

661 Don't let angry reactions to poor shots get the better of you—relax and breathe out the emotion.

662 Thinking too far ahead can prevent you from focusing on the shot at hand. Keep your mind in the present.

663 **Ten deep breaths before a shot can help to quieten the nerves.**

664 Apply your pre-shot routine for every shot.

665 If I had to pick a single reason why most people do not play golf well I would say it is the inability of their spirit to bounce back from adversity.

[GARY PLAYER]

666 Pretend each game is your last so you can let yourself enjoy it.

667 **Take care of the shots and the round will take care of itself.**

668 Golf is a game, not a matter of life or death.

669 Stay focused on the perfect landing area.

670 If you hit a terrible shot, take your time before the next. Recheck the problem, regroup your emotions, and refocus your concentration on the shot at hand.

671 **Nervous in front of others? Lighten up—everyone is.**

672 Predict your shots. You may not make them all, but you will benefit from the ones that you do.

673 Don't think about ends, think about the means of getting there.

674 If you are facing a pressure shot, say to yourself, "I have practiced hard to produce my best at moments like this." Trust in your preparation, check your grip, check your stance, aim, and fire.

[GARY PLAYER]

675 Stop yourself from fretting. Calm your emotions, rest your attention on the task at hand, think of your target, and play the shot.

676 **Only a fool lets anger spoil his fun.**

677 The physical and mental are intimately related. The more you practice correctly, the more unconscious the swing will be. The more unconscious the swing, the less your mind will interfere and the easier it will be to let go.

678 To calm your nerves before a match, lie down, close your eyes, and focus on relaxing each part of your body individually.

679 Sometimes you can settle butterflies in your tummy by filling it. Always take food with you on the course because feeding the belly can calm the mind.

680 **I have to spend as much time on the mental game as I do on the practice range.**

[TOM KIT]

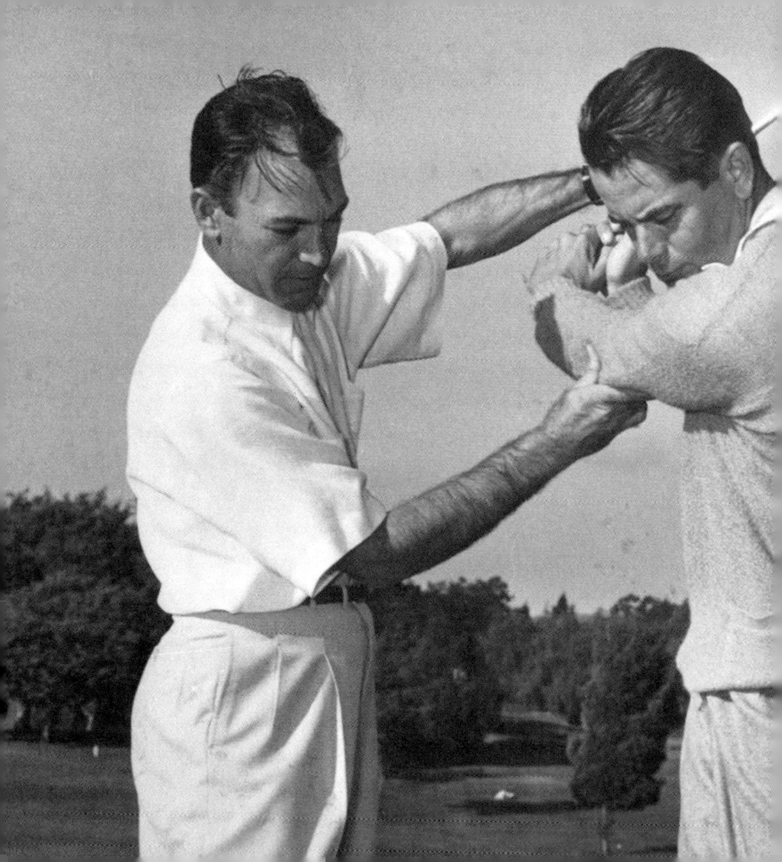

FIXES AND FITTINGS

681 The first rule of fault-fixing is to have a lesson.

682 The second rule of fault-fixing is do what the teacher tells you.

683 If you hit the ground before the ball, a fat shot, you may be crouching too low at address.

684 **Fat shots occur because excessive arm movement and a static body cause a choppy downward swing. Think about starting the downswing with a slight lateral movement of the hips toward the target.**

685 If you are topping the ball, you could be looking up too soon. Keep your head down until after the ball has gone.

686 **Prevent head movement—try practicing with the sun behind you and watch your shadow.**

687 **Head movement can cause fat shots. A downward head movement causes the right shoulder to drop. Try thinking of the head as the pivot of the swing around which all the action takes place.**

688 Too much lateral head movement causes loss of balance. Try to keep the head behind the ball until after impact.

689 Properly fitted clubs are the only part of improved golf that money can buy.

[TOMMY ARMOUR]

690 Fat shots can be caused by the hands separating at the top of the backswing. Practice with a blade of grass placed between the top of your left thumb and your right palm. The piece of grass will stay in place if you don't separate your hands.

691 **Remember that fat shots and hooks are due to poor synchronization between arms, hands, and body. Concentrate on unwinding the body as the arms come down.**

692 Always hooking? Check to see if either of your hands are too strong. A strong grip has the thumb knuckle joints pointing away from the target rather than straight upward.

693 A hook may be caused by an over-closed stance. Check that your feet are parallel with your shoulders and your back foot is not too far behind the target line.

694 Hooking can occur when the shoulders are closed to the target. To align them, lay a club across your chest, touching both shoulders, and make it point at the target.

695 To prevent a hook, ensure that your hips are turning correctly on the downswing. At impact, your belt buckle should be almost pointing at the target and your weight should be almost entirely on the front foot.

696 **To cure a strong grip, turn the hands counter-clockwise so the back of the left hand is pointing at the target.**

697 A common cause of slicing is an open stance where the front foot is back from the target line. Close your stance so that your belt buckle points at the ball.

698 If you have squared your feet and still slice the ball, check to see if your shoulders are aligned to the target.

699 If you hit too many shots out to the right, you could be tilting, not turning. Stick an umbrella in the ground next to your right foot and practice hitting shots without pushing it back with your leg. This will make you concentrate on rotating your hips.

700 A quick temporary fix for slicing is to close the clubface.

701

You may lose balance by shifting your weight too much to the left on the downswing. Flex the knees more at address and try to maintain a "sitting down" feeling throughout.

702 The smother, or excessively low shot, is due to the clubface being hooded at impact.

703 **One cause of a smother is a poor grip. Make sure your right hand is correctly positioned and not under the shaft.**

704 To stop a smother, ensure the left hand is not turned right over—ideally, you should only see two and a half knuckles of your left hand when you look at your grip at address.

705 If you have a correct grip and still smother, you may be rolling your wrist too much. This can only be checked by an observer or by seeing your swing on video.

706 A smother may be caused by an excessive lateral movement toward the target.

707 A pulled shot is one that goes straight left. If you pull consistently, you must be striking from the outside in.

708 **Poor alignment can cause a pull. Remember G.A.S.P: Grip, Stance, Aim, and Posture.**

709 To cure a pull, check that your backswing starts correctly with the left shoulder, arms, and clubhead moving in one piece.

710 **If the clubhead is out of line at the top of the backswing, you could pull the ball. Ask a friend to check that it is parallel to the target.**

711 To prevent pulling, keep the clubhead inside the intended line of flight on the downswing.

712 Are you pushing the shot out to the right? Your body may be swaying left as you come down. Think of getting your hands to the ball more quickly.

713

To cure a sway, practice standing with a golf ball under the outside of your right foot.

714

Topping can be caused by too much lateral movement in the lower body. Try to keep the head behind the ball at impact.

715 Hands separating at the top of the swing can cause you to hook the ball. Try gripping a little tighter with the right hand.

716 A skied ball off the tee is caused primarily by teeing the ball too high.

717 Topping off the tee? Check the tee height. Half the ball should be above the clubface at address.

718 An instant cure for smothering the driver is using a three wood. The loft will be reduced to that of a driver.

719 Keep the backswing low and slow to prevent skied shots with your woods.

720 A weak grip can cause you to sky your iron shots.

721 Skied irons can happen when the ball is too far forward in the stance.

722 Always skying your short irons? Your hands may be too far behind the ball at address.

723 A fast backswing can cause overswinging.

724 Overswinging is losing control at the top of the backswing. The primary cause among beginners is a bent left arm—keep it straight

725 If you delay cocking your wrists, you may overswing. Practice breaking the wrists early with a sand wedge and then transfer this feeling to other clubs.

726 **Overswinging can be caused by letting go at the top of the backswing. Grip firmly with the last three fingers of the left hand.**

727 Jerky or "quick" swings are commonly caused by anxiety. Relax at address and think "slow" as you make your swing.

728 To cure a jerky swing, practice hitting balls ridiculously slowly. You will be amazed by how far you still hit the ball.

729 If you lose your balance on your followthrough, poor weight distribution at address may be the problem. Check that your weight is not too far over your toes before you swing.

730 Shanking, or hitting the ball out of the heel of the club, is caused by many factors, but the most common is standing too close to the ball.

731 **The second most common cause of a shank is too flat a swing plane. Paradoxically this can result from being too far from the ball.**

732 To stop shanking, practice taking the clubhead straight back from the ball with the left shoulder passing under the right.

733 **If you have a bad case of the shanks, get a lesson from the pro.**

734 If you toe the ball, then logic tells you that you may be standing too far away from it.

735 Toeing the driver is most commonly caused by positioning the ball too far forward in your stance.

736 Scooping is due to lack of confidence. Trust the loft of the club to get the ball airborne.

737 To stop scooping, try to hit the ball low. Get the hands ahead of the clubface at impact.

738 Stop first-tee jitters by warming up before playing.

739 First-tee jitters make you forget the fundamentals—stay calm.

740 Take deep breaths as you stand up to hit your first shot.

741 Take your time on the first tee. Hurrying is the prime cause of disaster.

742 The primary swing thought on the first tee is to relax your forearms and shoulders.

743 Don't overpower the drive on the first tee.

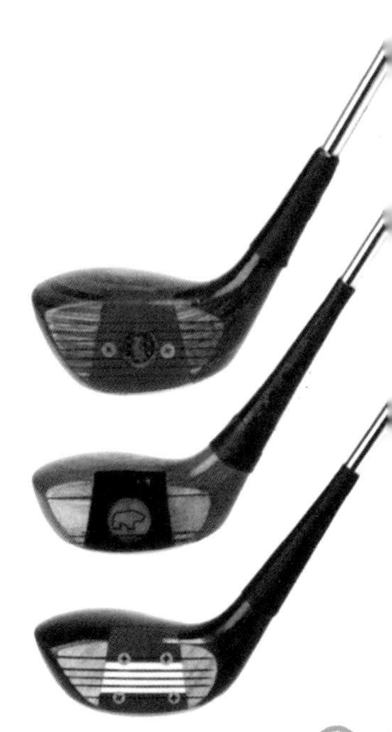

744 The lie angle of clubs—the angle that the shaft makes with the ground at address—has the most influence on accuracy. If the lie angle is too upright, the ball travels left. If it is too flat, the ball travels to the right.

745 **Adjusting lie angles is a relatively simple procedure. Ask your pro to check and, if necessary, alter them for you.**

746 Clubs that are too short may contribute to hitting the ball off the toe.

747 Clubs that are too long may cause you to hit the ball off the heel.

748 **If a shaft is too short, the lie angle will be too flat.**

749 **If the shaft is too long, the lie angle will be too upright.**

750 For golfers who prefer consistency and feedback, steel is the most common choice for shafts, but graphite is lighter and enables more clubhead speed.

751 Small, weak golfers play best with light clubs.

752 Tall, strong golfers gain better feel with heavy clubs.

753 **Golfers with a quick, snappy tempo benefit from light clubs.**

754 Golfers with long, slow tempos are better off using heavier clubs.

755 Different shafts flex in different places. The three main ones are: Low Kick Point—causes a high trajectory and a right-to-left shot; Mid Kick Point—causes a medium trajectory; High Kick Point—causes a low trajectory and a left-to-right shot.

756 Weaker, high-handicap golfers will prefer a low kick shaft while more advanced players will prefer a mid to high kick shaft.

757 **The correct flex requirement of a shaft is determined by clubhead speed—the greater the clubhead speed the stiffer the shaft required and visa versa—which is why ladies and juniors benefit from whippier shafts.**

758 A shaft that is too stiff results in lower ball flight, a left-to-right shot, and a harder feel.

759 A shaft that is too whippy results in a higher ball flight and a right-to-left shot.

760 "Offset" is the amount that the blade sits behind the shaft. The greater the offset the more it keeps the hands ahead of the ball at address, promoting accuracy for high handicappers.

761 Proper grip thickness creates better feel, distance, and control. The correct measure for a grip is for the tips of your fingers to just touch the palm of your left hand.

762 Very lofted drivers tend to encourage shots to travel from left-to-right.

763 Drivers with little or no loft tend to encourage right-to-left shots.

764 **A warm ball flies farther than a cold one—in winter keep them in your pocket.**

765 When your hands start to slip, renew your grips.

766 Most club golfers should have five woods in their bag. Long irons are just too hard to hit.

767 A seven wood is not only easier to hit than a three iron, it is also more versatile.

768 **Most golfers would be better off using the three wood off the tee than the driver.**

769 Have two pairs of golf shoes. Wear them alternately and clean them between rounds. They will last three times as long and remain waterproof.

770 Replace worn spikes and cleats (soft spikes) on your shoes.

771 Clean your clubs regularly.

772 Try before you buy any club.

773 Take advice from your pro as to which clubs will suit your game.

774 Are you constantly topping the ball? This could be caused by poor positioning of the ball at address. Ensure that it is inside the left heel.

775 It is worth spending the money to get good quality equipment.

776 The more expensive the ball, the better the feel.

777 Most amateurs cannot hit a three iron, so leave it out of the bag and carry an extra wedge.

778 The finer the sand, the more bounce you need on your sand wedge.

779 **If it is cold, take a hand warmer—cold hands limit feel during the swing.**

780 It is worth trying out several putters until you find one you click with.

781 Cavity-backed clubs are much easier to hit than blades.

782 Scrub your club grips in soapy water to keep them soft and tacky.

783 Buy a heavy club for practicing.

784 **Have two, three, or four putters and change them often. This will increase your sense of feel.**

785 Don't lean heavily on your clubs, especially if they are graphite shafted. It weakens them.

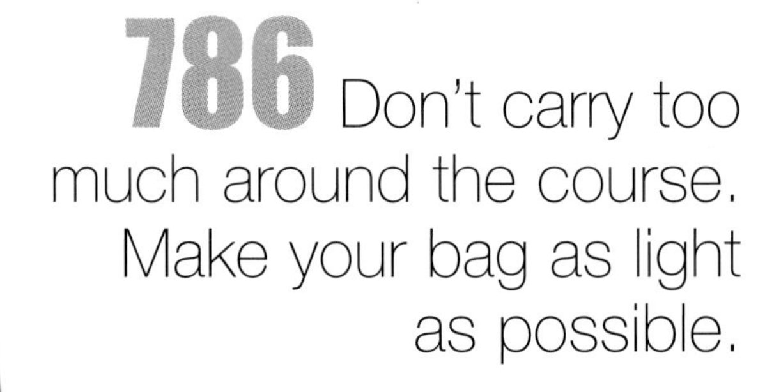

786 Don't carry too much around the course. Make your bag as light as possible.

787 **Invest in a lob wedge. It will save you shots.**

NEGOTIATING THE COURSE

788 More good rounds are spoiled through lack of care on the first hole than the last.

[HARRY VARDON]

789 **You have to think your way round a golf course.**

790 Arrive at the course early enough to warm up before your round.

791 Your pre-round warm up will tell you how you are hitting the ball that day.

792 Practice the short game if you are short of time before a match.

793 **Be as relaxed as possible when you arrive at the course—allow plenty of time to get there and listen to your favorite music in the car.**

794 Make sure you have everything you need before you set off for the course.

795 Be consistent with your pre-match preparation, it helps develop confidence.

796 If you are playing a strange course talk with the pros about its idiosyncrasies before you set off.

797 Putting warm-up: Forget mechanics and concentrate on rhythm, feel, and the speed of the greens.

798 Don't work on swing changes before a game.

799 If you arrive at the course with just a few minutes to warm up before a round, use the time to hit chip shots. The chip shot, being a short version of the full swing, tells your muscles and your golfing brain to get ready to play.

[HARVEY PENICK]

800 New to a course? Then buy a course plan.

801 Your first putts will most likely be long ones, so warm up with a few 25- to 50-foot putts.

802 **Hit a few two-foot putts. The sound of the ball dropping is good for the soul.**

803 Play for par over the first four holes, aiming to drop a maximum of one shot from your handicap—this will help to build confidence early in the round.

804 Plan your strategy from green to tee.

805 When in trouble, ask yourself where you would like to be playing the next shot from and whether the lie will allow you to reach it.

806 Be as precise in your aim as you would wish the result to be.

807 If the weather is bad, or the course is in poor condition, remember that the circumstances are the same for everyone. The best man will always win.

808 The course is your real opponent. It is the medium through which you measure yourself against your competitors, so make it your primary adversary.

809 The best way to beat trouble is to stay out of it. On the tee box, if there is trouble to the right, set up on the right of the tee and aim left. This gives you the maximum angle to avoid it.

810 Always calculate the yardage of approach shots.

811 **Irons for accuracy and distance control.**

812 **Woods for pure distance.**

813 To break 90, ignore pin positions and aim for the heart of every green.

814 **To break 80, focus on the short game.**

815 Memorize the distance you hit with every club in your bag.

816 **Don't always go for it. If the pin is situated behind a hazard, don't aim for it. Be sensible and aim for the center of the green.**

817 If your shot doesn't require a full swing, don't use one.

818 **The shorter the distance, the more important distance becomes.**

819 If you are a high handicapper, regard long par fours as par fives.

820 **Know your natural shot shape and learn to play with it.**

821 The prime objective in playing from rough is to minimize the club's contact with it. An upright swing achieves that objective better than a flat swing because of the sharper angle at which the clubhead rises and returns to the ball.

[JACK NICKLAUS]

822 Swing with ease into the breeze.

823 If you can hit the driver well—drive on.

824 If you can't hit the driver well—don't until you can.

825 **Always test the rough with a practice swing so you get an idea of how tough it will be to hit the real shot.**

826 If the rough is growing in the direction of the shot, the ball will come out faster; if it is against the direction, the grass will resist the club, so you must swing harder.

[RAY FLOYD]

827 **Keep shoulders parallel to the ground on uphill and downhill lies.**

828 On a downhill lie, keep some of your weight on the upper foot and play the ball a little forward of your stance.

829 **If the ball is above your feet, it will probably draw or hook. Open the clubface a little to add fade spin to counteract the draw.**

830 Swing smooth and easy on awkward lies and don't over-swing.

831 If the ball is below your feet, it will have a tendency to fade or slice. Close the clubface to add draw spin to counteract the slice.

832 If you have to hit the ball high over trees, remember to use the club with the required loft. Concentrate on hitting down behing the ball and keep your weight on your back foot.

833 Too much ambition is a bad thing to have for the golfer in trouble.

[BOBBY JONES]

834 **Memorize the yardages on your local course.**

835 If you need to keep the ball low, to go under tree branches, for example, but need distance, play the ball back in your stance.

836 Think safety first from deep sand traps—just make sure you get out.

837 When the ball is in a fairway sand trap, dig your feet into the sand to get a stable base but grip down the club to compensate for being closer to the ball.

838 To successfully hit a shot from a fairway sand trap, place more weight on your front foot. Keep the wrists supple, take a full shoulder turn, and swing through.

839 To keep balanced in a fairway sand trap, let your knees pinch toward each other so the majority of your weight is over the inside of your feet.

840 The secret to good sand play is to minimize movement in the feet and legs.

841 Don't let the clubface close when in the sand. Keep your right palm facing the target and accelerate through the ball to a full finish.

842 Draw the ball by swinging the club a little more inside on the backswing.

843 To promote a draw, try making your grip stronger by rolling your hands backward in minute increments. Use trial-and-error as you rotate to different positions.

844 **To hit the ball low, keep your hands ahead of the clubhead for the whole swing.**

845 The draw has more roll. It fights an opposing crosswind and will help you bend a shot from right to left around an obstruction.

846 Don't play your wedge in a crosswind—it will be hard to control the ball.

847 Keep yourself warm in winter. Wear long johns, a hat, and use a hand warmer.

848 Woods are more consistent than irons off wet fairways. Irons have a tendency to get stuck in the soggy grass.

849 **Don't fight the wind—use it to shape your shots.**

850 **When the greens are really wet, aim shots right up to the flag if you hit a lofted club because the ball will plug on impact.**

851 Putts break less on wet greens.

852 **The ball will run on hard, dry fairways, but remember it can also run into trouble.**

853 **Use a wedge to putt from the collar of thick fringe around the greens. Try to hit the ball dead center with the edge of the wedge.**

854 If the ground is hard, move the ball slightly back in your stance to ensure good contact.

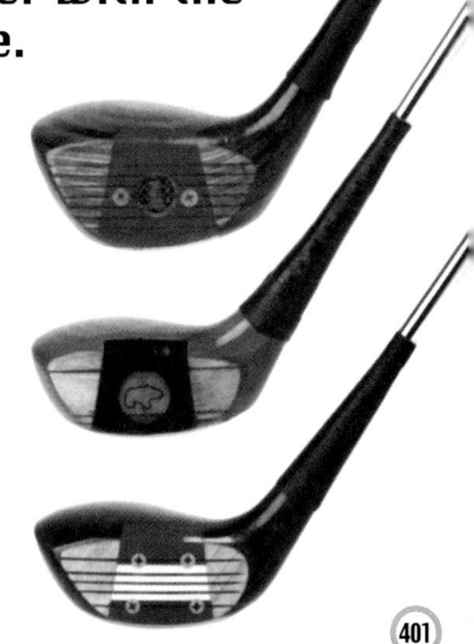

855 If your ball lands in the center of a divot, play a normal shot but keep the ball slightly back in your stance and think of hitting down on the ball.

856 **If your ball is resting in the side of a divot farthest from you, close the face slightly to avoid the toe catching the grass.**

857 If the ball is resting on the side of a divot nearest to you, open the face slightly to avoid catching the heel on the grass.

858 When playing off leaves or pine needles, don't ground your club. There is a danger of moving the ball and incurring a penalty shot.

859 In heavy rough the club will tend to close before impact, as the grass wraps around it. Open the face to compensate.

860 **The ball will stop very quickly on wet greens. To guarantee more roll, use a less lofted iron to approach them.**

861 Check the tree line. If you hit above it, the wind may affect your shot.

862 When driving downwind, use a three wood. It gives more control than a driver.

863 **When driving against the wind, use your driver to get the distance but tee it low so the ball will travel under the wind.**

864 To hit a driver off the fairway, grip down the shaft, imagine it's your three wood, and swing slowly. Practice this before trying it on the course.

865 Hitting a driver off the fairway is an excellent shot into the wind.

866 To play a low punch shot, keep your weight on your front foot.

867 To make the ball stop quickly on punch shots, keep your clubface square for as long as you can during followthrough.

868 When in heather don't try to leather!

869 **Slightly lengthen your putting stroke against the wind.**

870 Wear plenty of thin layers in the cold—less bulk aids easy swinging.

871 **Check the yardage from the tee. The tee markers may have been moved from the actual distance disc.**

872 Think to make pars on the fives and threes.

873 **Most par threes are protected by sand traps at the front edge so always err on the long side.**

874 If the ground is hard, try to keep your hands ahead of the ball for a clean contact.

875 Play the safest shot you can every time.

876 Don't be ashamed to hit a wood on a par three.

877 **Short par fours have a design feature to make them difficult—accuracy is more important than distance.**

878 **Distance is more important than direction on approach shots. Always take enough club to get to the hole.**

879 On long par fours, don't hit a driver if the fairway is tight. It is better to have a 200-yard shot from the fairway than to hack out of the woods forty yards closer to the hole.

880 **On par fives there is no real advantage to hitting a driver if you can't get to the green with your second shot.**

881 Find your favorite wedge shot. If you can confidently hit a wedge 100 yards, try to leave yourself that distance from the hole as often as you can.

882 Against the wind, from uphill lies, and in very cold or wet weather, take one more club than you think you will need.

883 Always use a tee on par threes. Air has less resistance than dirt.

[JACK NICKLAUS]

884 **If you can't easily carry a hazard, don't try it.**

885 **Set yourself a little goal, such as making a set number of pars or not three putting, and concentrate on achieving it.**

886 On-course nutrition is important. Take snack bars, bananas, or dried fruit to keep up your energy levels.

887 Hydration is important. Take plenty of water with you and drink throughout the round.

888 Choose your favorite club in pressure situations.

889 Hit the shot you know you can hit, not the one you want to.

890 Be aware of where the trouble is, but forget that it is there.

891 Knowing where you want the ball to go is better than thinking where it shouldn't.

892 **Split your rounds into six mini-rounds. Set yourself a target for each three holes of the course.**

893 **Don't be too bold on doglegs—even the pros don't always try to shape their shots round them.**

894 **Establish the best way to play each hole on your home course and plan your game accordingly.**

895 Stop before making a shot if your set up does not feel right—stand back, refocus, and then set yourself correctly.

896 Learning from your mistakes means not making them twice.

PRACTICE TO BE PERFECT

897 "Never had a lesson in my life" is a phrase uttered with smug satisfaction by a good many people. The correct reply is, of course, "That's why you are no better than you are."

[HENRY LONGHURST]

898 **Practice ranges and putting greens are there for experimentation before you try it out for real.**

899 Don't be afraid to hit poor shots in practice.

900 Practice making swings without your wrists. Dead hands make good shots under pressure.

901 To get a sense of exactly where on the clubface your ball connects, stick a piece of sticky tape on it in practice. When you hit the ball it will leave an impression on the tape.

902 Every day you don't hit balls is one day longer it will take you to get better.

[BEN HOGAN]

903 If you are playing a practice round and not holding anyone up, hit extra shots.

904 Hit putts from all over the green to get an idea of the overall contours.

905 **A practice round is just a round to get the feel of the course.**

906 Hit balls on the practice range only until you start to feel tired—don't overdo it.

907 When you are at the practice range, learn how far you hit each club.

908 Always practice to a target. Play the course on the range.

[GARY PLAYER]

909 Practice your pre-shot routine on the practice range.

910 **Always take time to practice the shots that you find most difficult.**

911 **When practicing, think keep it smooth.**

912 Start a practice session with your wedge to loosen up.

913 The player who expects a lesson to “take” without subsequent practice just isn’t being honest with himself or fair to his professional.

[GARY PLAYER]

914 **Try to play with players better than you.**

915 Don’t just slash away with the driver on the practice ground.

916 All my life I have tried to hit practice shots with a purpose. I always practice as I intend to play and there is a limit to the number of shots you can hit effectively before losing your concentration.

[JACK NICKLAUS]

917 Always practice with a club on the ground aiming at the target to act as an alignment guide. This will ingrain a correct set up and aim position into your psyche.

918 Use a video camera and study your swing from time to time.

919 The secret is digging dirt.

[BEN HOGAN]

920 When you are at the practice range, pretend you are playing a round of golf at your home course. Start with the driver and then hit the iron you would need to play on the first hole and so on.

921 Don't regard practice as a routine—vary your practice sessions.

922 Always practice with a purpose.

923 Quality not quantity is the key to good practice.

924 Practice does not make perfect, it makes permanent. Only perfect practice makes perfect.

925 Cure a slice—practice hitting shots with your feet together.

926 Never practice your full swing when the wind is blowing into your back. This will make you swing across the ball and hit from the top.

[HARVEY PENICK]

927 Golf-specific exercises designed to increase strength and flexibility are essential. Ask a personal trainer to design a program for you.

928 Dedicated practice reaps rewards.

929 The repetitive nature of swinging a club can cause injury—beware of doing too much.

930 The stress placed on your spine when you swing is more than 600 percent greater than that of standing upright, so rest frequently.

931 Posture, balance, flexibility, strength, and conditioning all affect the way you swing the club. They must all work well together if you want to hit the ball with distance, accuracy, and consistency as well as to avoid injury.

932 Lower back pain is usually caused by tight, inflexible muscles in the hips and lower back coupled with weak abdominal muscles. Focus on strengthening those areas.

933 Shoulder, wrist, and elbow pain are often caused by tight muscles when you grip too tightly—loosen the grip a little.

934 **To warm up, walk around a little, slowly swinging and circling your arms.**

935 After stretching, begin by practicing putting, then hit a few with an eight or nine iron to loosen up.

936 **Use this stretch to improve posture: With one hand on the top of your club and one hand on the bottom, hold it vertically down your back and press it against your spine. Tighten your stomach muscles and bend forward into an address posture. Hold the position for six to eight seconds. Repeat 20 to 30 times.**

937 To loosen the lower spine, place the driver across the back of your neck, hands on the head and grip. Pivot the club around the top of the spine. Do this slowly and deliberately and repeat 20 to 30 times.

938 Don't become a range star. If you focus on practicing your long game, you might get addicted to hitting long drives and neglect your short game.

939

Loosen up by sitting on the edge of a chair and slowly swiveling your upper body to your right until you feel mild tension. Then grab the back of your seat, keeping your feet on the floor, and hold the stretch for three seconds. Repeat on the left side.

940 A good stretch is to hold a club at both ends, with arms outstretched. Feet shoulder width apart. Bend forward to touch your toes and hold for a count of three. Now rise up and bend over backwards until you feel the stretch in you lower back. Hold for a count of five and repeat twice more.

941 Do a couple of back bends after each hole to regain the arch in the lower back.

942 To counteract constant rotation in the same direction, swing in the opposite direction from time to time to loosen the joints in the lower back.

943 Learn correct balance. If you're not balanced during the swing, your spine isn't free to rotate over the hips and you'll put extra stress on the lower back and shoulders.

944 Make the last shot you hit in warm-up the first you hit on the tee.

[KEN VENTURI]

945 Practice chipping into an upturned umbrella.

946 Practice little and often rather than a lot at one time.

947 Don't practice in the rain, but practice while wearing your rain gear from time to time.

948 To stop "flicking" under the ball when chipping or putting, practice wearing a tennis wristband on the left wrist and tuck the end of the grip underneath it. This will prevent your wrist from breaking.

949 **Prevent yourself from hitting with only your favorite clubs—leave them at home.**

950 Always aim at a specific target on the range.

951 **Don't practice full swings in high winds.**

952 Keep a record of your performance on the course in order to know what you need to practice.

953 For every fault there is a remedy.

954 **Practice in proportion to the shots you take. You should spend the most time on your putts, about the same on your chips, pitches, and sand play, and the least on the long game.**

955 **Ask yourself why you are practicing. If you don't know the answer, you shouldn't be doing it.**

956 You can improve your golf by watching television. Close observation of the best players in the game will reap rewards.

957 **Go through your pre-shot routine with at least 20 percent of your practice shots.**

958 Hitting off mats is not ideal but it is better than nothing.

959 Learn to hit each club in turn, starting with the easiest. You will master them all in time.

960 Try to make your practice as real as possible. Set targets such as hitting three wedges to within three feet of a pin. Start again if you do not make it.

961 **At the range, try to make each shot a good one—as if it really counted.**

962 When practicing sand shots, place the ball in the middle of a scorecard and practice hitting the sand behind the scorecard to get used to taking the right amount.

963 Finish on a high—stop practicing when you've holed a putt.

964 Practice chipping at home on the carpet with light plastic practice balls.

965 Experiment at the range—practice different stances and different swing lengths to familiarize yourself with shot making.

966 Practice short putts as much as you can. If holing six-footers is second nature, you will be more successful on the course.

967 If you feel the urge to practice, give in to it.

968 Practice pitching over bunkers to hone your feel for distance.

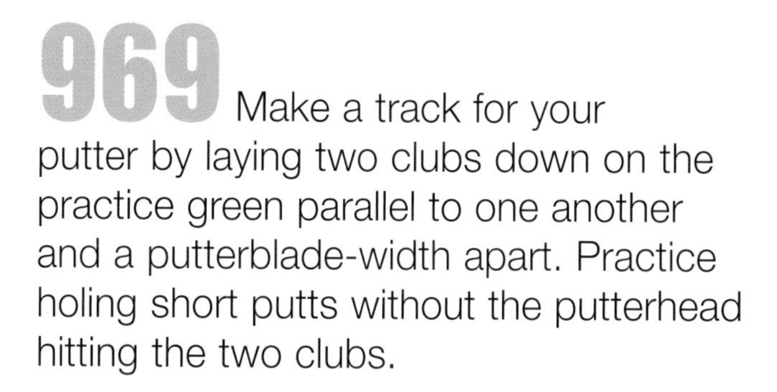

969 Make a track for your putter by laying two clubs down on the practice green parallel to one another and a putterblade-width apart. Practice holing short putts without the putterhead hitting the two clubs.

970 The part shot from 50 to 60 yards out is golf's "money shot." When warming up before playing, always devote time to 60-yard shots, even if that's all you do.

[JIM FLICK]

971 **If you don't want to practice, don't make yourself.**

972 **Make yourself visualize each practice shot before you make it.**

973 Simply hitting balls rather then thinking about each shot leads to complacency and poor habits.

974 **You learn more from your misses than your good shots.**

975 Make a point of practicing your putting when out on the course.

976 **Test your reading skills on a wide variety of greens.**

977 Improvement tends to come in spurts. Be prepared for long, frustrating weeks when nothing seems to get better.

978 If you are practicing hard and not improving, maybe you need a lesson.

979 **The practice tee is the place to try things out and to try hard; the golf course the place to let things go, free yourself up. Don't try harder on the course. Try less hard.**

[DAVIS LOVE, JR.]

980 To make yourself extend fully on your drives, try hitting balls teed-up six to 10 inches to the left of where you would normally hit them.

981 **Place a tee in the ground two feet behind your teed ball. Try making your backswing touch the tee as you go back.**

982 Train yourself to hit through the ball by placing a second tee six inches in front of your ball and try to catch it on your followthrough.

983 To build body awareness, try hitting balls with stiff legs and then let them adopt the normal stance. Note how different each stance feels.

984 **The best time to practice is right after a round, when the mistakes are fresh in your mind.**

[TOM WATSON]

985 Before practicing hitting balls, swing a club 10 to 20 times without a ball but pick a spot on the ground and try to hit it every time.

986 Rate your confidence on each type of shot from one to 10—one being no confidence, 10 being very confident. Practice those shots that score lowest.

987 **Don't use range balls to practice chips and putts; use the ball you normally use when playing.**

988 **Focus on one goal at a time and one change at a time.**

989 Get feedback—a video lesson is the most effective way to improve.

990 Mix it up on the range—don't go into "remote control."

991 **Don't spend too much time on the range—you must play on the course to reap the benefits.**

992 Force yourself to practice from odd lies and strange positions.

993 Spend time practicing in the rough and in sand traps.

994 Practice with a partner and set yourself contests to make it more interesting.

995 On practice rounds, hit three balls off the tee and choose the worst one for your second.

996 In practice, 20 meaningful strokes are better than 200 bashed balls.

997 Experiment by using different clubs to hit the same distances.

998 Have a routine in your practice. Start with the wedges and work through the set. Do odd-numbered irons one day, evens the next.

999 **Make a habit of practicing at the driving range on those long winter nights. It is a good time to work on changes to your swing.**

1000 The harder you work, the luckier you get.

[GARY PLAYER]

FURTHER READING

- *Bobby Jones Golf Tips* edited by Sidney L. Matthew (Sleeping Bear Press, 1999)

- *The Complete Golfer* by Harry Vardon (Fredonia Books, 2001)

- *Dave Pelz's Putting Bible* by Dave Pelz (Doubleday, 2000)

- *Dave Pelz's Short Game Bible* by Dave Pelz (Broadway Books, 1999)

- *Exercise Guide to Better Golf* by Frank Jobe, Lewis Yocum, Robert Mottram, and Marylin Pink (Human Kinetics, 1995)

- *Five Lessons: The Modern Fundamentals* of Golf by Ben Hogan (Fireside, 1985)

- *Golf is Not a Game of Perfect* by Dr. Bob Rotella (Simon & Schuster, 1995)

- *The Golf Swing* by David Leadbetter (Stephen Greene Press, 1990)

- *The Golfer's Guide to the Meaning of Life* by Gary Player (Rodale Press, 2001)
- *The Inner Game of Golf* by Timothy Gallwey (Random House,1998)
- *Mental Management for Great Golf* by Dr Bee Epstein-Shepherd (McGraw-Hill/Contemporary Books, 1998)
- *Peak Performance Golf* by Patrick Cohn Phd. (McGraw-Hill/ Contemporary Books, 2000)
- *Putting Out of Your Mind* by Dr Bob Rotella (Free Press, 2001)

PICTURE CREDITS

p.8: © Royalty-Free/CORBIS. p.60: © Bettmann/CORBIS. p.130: © Paul Barton/CORBIS. p.200: © Rick Gayle/CORBIS. p.264: © Duomo/CORBIS. p.322: © Bettmann/CORBIS. p.372: © Getty Images. p.418: © Chris Trotman/NewSport/CORBIS.

Published by MQ Publications Limited
12 The Ivories
6–8 Northampton Street
London, N1 2HY
email: mail@mqpublications.com
website: www.mqpublications.com

Copyright © 2004 MQ Publications Limited
Text copyright © 2004 Stephen Wilkinson PhD

Editor: Tracy Hopkins
Designer: Lindsey Johns

ISBN: 1-84072-4870

10 9 8 7 6 5 4 3 2 1

All rights reserved. No part of this publication may be used or reproduced or transmitted in any form or by any means, electronic or mechanical, including photocopy, recording, or any information storage and retrieval system now known or to be invented without permission in writing from the publishers.

Printed and bound in China